Around the World by Mistake

Around the World by Mistake

Jane Winslow Eliot

CONTENTS

1. GREECE

The Message

Alex had been lying in the hammock under the ancient olive tree in front of our tiny house on Corfu Island in Greece. I was sitting nearby on an old upturned wine barrel, savoring the fragrant blend of thyme, orange blossoms, and fresh salt air. The children's voices reached over to us from the stony beach where they played on a decaying caique – a Greek fishing vessel drying in the sun.

Our cottage on the shores of northern Corfu was tucked in an orange grove overlooking a sparkling Greek bay. Activities were fishing boats at dawn, delivery of the morning milk to our door in the cow itself, ear-shattering thunderstorms, and a climbable galleon-sized wreck rotting on the beach at the foot of the garden. Our two youngsters, seven and eight years old, spoke Greek like natives and had been incorporated into a gang of Greek children ranging in age from six to sixteen. In return I taught them all painting and sculpture.

I watched their angular silhouettes move like dancers against a backdrop of blue sky and even bluer water, water which barely whispered in the still summer afternoon. Crickets and tree frogs hummed loudly.

"We should send the children to school next year," Alex said.

"What for?" I asked. "They're learning more living here in Greece and playing with the other kids than they'd ever learn in school."

"There's more to school than learning about life. There's reading, math, history, geography," Alex answered, making the plausible kind of sense that leads to argument.

There had been no argument between us, however. Neither of us cared to corral Jeff and Wyd into school just yet. We wanted them to experience life as a fish in water, or ourselves part of the air we breathe. We wanted to foster the children's tiny harmonies by tuning them into the larger harmonies of our earth globe. We wished to help them escape the narrows of nationality, religion, class, in order to take part in a whole universe as whole people. They were earthlings, standing on top of their own spinning world, reaching for their own brass rings.

"When they get old enough I wish they'd get jobs as cabin boys and girls and go around the world," I mused, the vision of the world's wonders creating a longing in my soul. "I'd like them to experience that it really is round."

"We could buy them a globe now," Alex offered.

"It's not the same," I said. "Anyway, it would be great for them not to have dark blotches in their minds where India and China ought to be. Once they're in school they'll never be able to learn anything."

"If we didn't put them in school for another year," – Alex has a way of getting to the point sometimes, not wanting it to be left out – "We could take them around the world ourselves."

"When?" I asked

"This autumn?"

"I looked at that freighter paperback we bought last winter," I said, eager to hold onto this trend. "There's a Yugoslav boat, the only inexpensive one anywhere, that goes to Japan and back. It takes about seven months, up to sixteen passengers, and costs about $2,500 for the four of us."

I had looked it up last week.

Alex stretched comfortably, happy at the practical turn conversation had taken and that things seemed to have worked out without undue exertion. Sitting at his typewriter most of the day, he liked that. Although we had not made other plans, we knew we were leaving our Greek house for the winter, since the owner-fisherman would need to move back in for the rainy season. He and his family camped out in the orange grove for the summer and fall, but by October they'd need more shelter.

We had been living in Greece the past four years because we loved it there. I had worked at CBS with Edward R. Morrow and at *Time Magazine* as a researcher in Foreign Affairs and other departments. Alex had been Art Editor for *Time* for the past fifteen years, and now, a freelance journalist, wrote books and articles, mostly about art and mythology. We lived simply but our lives were textured. We could do odd things because we traveled light. A long freighter trip to the Far East would give us more time. The prospect of this new adventure filled me with delight. We knew the children's education would have to take priority at some point, eventually pulling us back to the States. But I dreaded suburbia, children in school, Alex commuting to the alcoholic austerity of 1960s New York, me in limbo. More immediately, it solved the problem of rent, food, and all other basics for at least seven months. By then new royalties and advances should be coming through and all would be well.

Fingers crossed.

It was the summer of 1963. We assumed that as Americans, two writers and two children, we would be welcomed on a freighter delivering goods to all manner of ports scattered across a restless world. Confidently, we mailed our reservation money for four tickets, two cabins. We left sufficient funds to cover the month until departure, plus the four-day drive to Yugoslavia for sailing. There was also enough left over to plan some short side trips when the ship was scheduled to load or off-load for days or even weeks at some exotic port.

Energetically we got visas for all our projected stops, including, I insisted, multiple visas when more than one stop was scheduled for a single country, such as India and Japan. The captain could authorize day passes at each port, but my mother's remembered warning spoke loudly inside my head: "Don't ever go any place from which you can't walk home."

Summer wore on. Each day passed saturated in island beauty and tender activities with the children. Then one chilly night Alex and I opened our trunk and got out the winter blankets. As we listened to the odd-sized bronze neck-bells on the goats pour rivers of sound through the open window, one firefly landed on our blanket. Blinking in a come-hither manner, it wandered about as if on the savannah. It worked. Before long, a new light semaphored its longings as they edged closer to each other. Tiny fulgurations led to intimacy: they began to synchronize their blinks. For the next several nights they met over our toes, turning on and off in happy unison.

I was inspired to read up on bugs. Their individual idiosyncrasies, the experts reported, was matched only by their uncanny ability to work together across vast distances – vast from an insect's point of view. I learned to hold my scrubbing hand in check – and watch. Over the next few weeks I found a rich world. First, ants in the kitchen. I got them out by clapping the lids of the frying pans over their heads. We saw scorpions doing their mating dance on the loose stone walls in our field. The shy, if deadly, creatures kept us from sitting on fragile walls, which would have been badly damaged. We saw the elusive trapdoor spider tunneling straight into the earth, dropping its tight-fitting, moss-covered door over its head to remain invisible. The islanders claimed these spiders were only invisible to adults. The naturalist Gerald Durrell wrote he had never seen one. Our kids showed us the trap doors.

One evening, sitting under our olive tree, watching as nothing at all happened all around us, the calm was shattered by a flash from the top of a chamomile blossom. A firefly sending semaphores.

4

Something had changed.

Soon there were two in the yard, their dainty dazzles beckoning from the marjoram stalks. They twinkled light and dark in sympathetic syncopations: two little lumens once again in rapture. The next night there were hundreds of thousands. The dark glimmered as giddy gadabouts gyrated over the oregano and barnstormed the wild thyme. They gleamed around the village well. Silver surfers rolled the luminous waves along the black sand beaches of an otherwise motionless black bay. They blinked along the narrow, empty road that passed in front of our house. We strolled along with the steady slowness of sleepwalkers, while fairy chariots glided out of our way. Like miniature meteor showers, the bugs blazed behind us and flared in front. As far as the eye could reach, flying up to fifteen or twenty feet, they traded glimmery communications against a backdrop of stars and phosphorescent water.

As the nights passed, they began to synchronize in pairs. At first a couple per field, or mountain path, or pebbly beach. Next night, twenty pairs blinking to their private tunes. Over the week they were finding each other by the hundreds, thousands, hundreds of thousands, couples slowly turning on and off and on. Soon all the fireflies in this bug-bedazzled dark had found a mate whose private music matched its own. The glister was anarchic, each twosome for itself.

One silvery dusk this too changed. Pair joined lustrous pair to blink in tiny soul trains. We four climbed our mountain to watch the new firefly-works from a crest overlooking the spectacle below. Lightning bugs undulated for miles. By the millions, they rocked in groups encompassing entire fields, each field flickering to its own secret rhythm. Finally, fields began to share one beat until holdouts along the perimeters threw in their phosphors and all blinked in synch.

We watched mesmerized until midnight, as dangerous shards of lightning tore the sky between Albania and us. Then, heading down the stream of cool fire, never rippling, never touching, something in ourselves synchronized with the pulsing pairs.

We got inside just before the downpour. Sheet lightning showed us branches breaking and wildflowers crumpling. Thunder crashed over our heads like frying pans of the gods. Next evening not one firefly had escaped alive to greet us.

For who had been the show, to what end the splendid spangle, we could not guess. But by this time we knew that bugs being bugs, they would be back on Corfu next spring, as they had for thousands of years, each one given his – or her – chance to blink in synch with the stars.

But we would not be there to greet them.

We understood the message. For us, too, it was time for things to change. What we had learned from Greece we would take with us. Like gypsies, we would wrap ourselves in experience, blankets around the soul, and now move on.

2. RIJECKA

We Board

We arrived on the docks of Rijecka, subdued with excitement. The autumn sun warmed our backs. No one was about. The harbor was stilled for lunchtime.

Confidently clasping my hands, the children looked around for the scruffy black freighter that was to carry us from Yugoslavia to Japan and back. We assumed it would look somewhat similar to the freighter we had sailed on from New York to Greece four years before. Alex put down the typewriter and the suitcase that held the things we couldn't afford to lose: toothbrushes, manuscripts, clock. I carried my purse and my camera. The two trunks were still in the car.

"There!" Jeff exclaimed, his voice low and thrilled. "That's her, isn't it?"

Squinting into the low afternoon sun, our eyes followed his finger pointing to a spectacular white vessel. Alex shook his head. Then, in disbelief, he read the ship's name out loud: Jessenice.

"Yes, there she is, kids. That's our new home." There was a mixture of puzzlement and relief in his tone.

Together we had pored over pictures that had been sent to us of the ship, but even so we were not prepared for her modern magnificence. Wedding cake white and sleek as a knife, she towered over her pudgy, work-blackened sisters.

Picking up the suitcase, Alex led the way to the gangplank.

We hesitated at the bottom, wondering if we could go aboard. Automatically Alex felt in his jacket pocket and pulled out our papers: passports, visas, medical certificates, money; all seemed to be in order.

Jeff tugged my arm. "There's the water line."

"That's it," Alex agreed.

"What's a water line?" Wyd asked eagerly. Golden freckles glowed in her face and she began to bounce with excitement.

In return for her older brother's explanation, she pointed out some sparrows perched on the deck railing, watching us with a good deal of chattery speculation. Jeff was nicely dressed in tailored short pants, dress shirt and tie, and a wool blazer we had bought him in Ireland. Over some objections, Alex had worn his Harris tweed, with a woven tie of matching colors we had bought from Vienoula on Mykonos.

His looking imposing had always made me feel secure when asking for a good table from head-waiters; a good room from hotel registrars; a front row ticket for the Paris opera; and, now, two cabins for a long trip handed out by the purser.

I can't remember what I wore. I know I must have been wearing low-heeled sandals because I never wore high-heels, ever. My brown hair would have been loose, because it always was. It reached down to my waist, full, strong, bronze. Alex called it chestnut with glints of gold, which made me feel rather proud of it, and he jealously kept people's hands off it. The rest would have been dignified but casual, and hand-woven; probably in blue.

8

From on high came a shout. Looking up we saw a tall, thin man leaning over the ship's railing at the top of the long gangplank. Black hair threaded with grey haloed his head. His soft white skin sagged over long bones, like a slightly large suit on a hanger. A white jacket flapped over black trousers shiny with age, his long legs ending in heavy black shoes half of which poked over the edge of the deck. Their black rubber soles were designed to last a lifetime. He seemed to be made of separate pieces. His smile, even from afar, was a keyboard of ivory alternating with black interstices. Thrusting bony wrists out into the air, he spread his long arms as if to embrace us, then beckoned us aboard.

We met at the top of the gangplank. His eyes were black and sad, and lit with the pale glow of kindness. He told us he was the ship's steward.

"My name is Stefan," he said, smiling down at the children. "I am responsible for the passengers."

No one else seemed to be around. The children's pattering footsteps echoed down silent, sun-filled corridors as Stefan led us to our adjoining cabins.

"Ah, we're at the back of the ship," I said.

"The stern," Jeff corrected me.

We showed our delight with the large cabins, each of which held two comfortable beds, a couch, an armchair, a bureau, and a working-size desk. Each had a private bathroom and enormous closets in an entrance hall. Through the portholes we could see one whole side of the port, silent and motionless as it slept through the afternoon siesta. Sailboats were still on the calm blue harbor waters.

Alex and I looked at each other, bemused by the unexpected luxury of freighter life.

Inviting us to follow him, Stefan showed us proudly around the inside of the passenger deck. Two corridors, shining with highly polished brass rails, emergency gongs, and handsome light-fixtures, ran the back half of the ship's inside length. Between them there was the dining room, the pantry, and the lounge. This was Stefan's domain.

"Just remember, children," he smiled, "you are on the right side of the ship. You can always tell where you are by remembering the motion of the ship. Face the front, feel your feet going forward, and your side is on your right hand."

"The other side is called port side, Mum," Jeff said, "because you always see the port from that side." He was excited. "Wyd, the front is called the prow."

Four large cabins opened on the right side ("It's called starboard, because you can see the stars better from that side.") and four more portside. As we looked over the other six cabins, all identical, I wondered who our fellow passengers would be. I had a sudden, almost imperceptible urge to flee, for large as it might seem now, our majestic white vessel might turn out to be a small thing in which to bob atop the waters of the world for seven whole months. Space has a peculiar way of stretching and shrinking at unexpected moments.

Wyd took hold of Stefan's long fingers, which brought a gentle smile to his face. His whole frame relaxed slightly as he showed us further forward to the dining room, set to accommodate thirteen people at four square tables. Large windows overlooked the back loading deck. On the left of the entrance, a door opened onto a tiny pantry. Across, a glass door opened onto the lounge.

"We serve tea in the lounge at four o'clock every afternoon. Dinner will be at six." Stefan addressed the children affectionately, making it a personal invitation into his kingdom rather than merely the ship's schedule.

We all thanked him.

"If you have any problem or questions you come to me," Stefan went on, "not the captain. He is responsible for the ship. I am responsible for the passengers. I see you at four-o'clock tea time." He straightened to smile at Alex and me. "Welcome aboard. I hope you will enjoy your journey."

He walked away along the sunny corridor, black and white clothes flapping, his head held high.

We proceeded to explore the rest of the ship. We crossed the dining room, passed Stefan's pantry, and went into the sun-filled lounge, silent and empty now. Three couches were set at right angles to each other in the center of the room. Two large tables with several packs of cards and one unopened game were spread out on their shiny surfaces, and several comfortable armchairs were arranged in a friendly way near the walls. The furniture, all bolted to the floor, was of bleached wood, covered with mellow beige and gold fabrics occasionally stroked by a brush of burnt orange. The afternoon sun poured through plate-glass windows that stretched the length of the room, overlooking the deserted loading deck. Opposite, a double door opened out onto the starboard side of the passenger's deck, also warmed now by the afternoon sun. The only gloomy touch was the huge photograph of Tito gazing forbiddingly from the lounge wall.

We stepped over the foot-high threshold and went outside.

The passenger deck spanned the middle of the ship, with three decks expanding below and three tapering above. Two gaping half-loaded holds were astern, and a third was still empty, looking like a deep, black hole in the deck. As we wandered forward we could see two more black holes ready for closing. This loading deck was where the crew lived. The kitchen was almost below the waterline and the hold reached well below that. Immediately above us the officers had their quarters. The bridge was next, and a small lookout deck topped it all off. We got to this funnel-forested overlook via the bridge deck that was open to passengers.

Jeff led us up the steep iron ladder-like stairs, with Wyd second, me third, and Alex ready to catch us if we stumbled. We found that the officers' deck was the sundeck as well. Deckchairs for the passengers were already set out for us, and we felt welcomed onto what seemed a friendly, intimate, well-kept ship.

Up another steep flight to the bridge. The wheelhouse was locked and deserted, but from its side we looked over the forward decks. Sailors had emerged from their rest and were beginning to clang the great iron hatches shut, locking them securely with enormous iron bolts and chains. At right angle to the bridge lay a magnificent radio room. Used to radar and radio and not much else on a freighter, when we looked through the closed, large plate-glass windows we were impressed at finding more electronic equipment than we had ever seen in one place before. The room was large, locked, fairly dark, and empty. Three walls were floor to ceiling with dials, blinking lights, knobs, buttons, and wires. One chair and a table were covered with charts – the only furniture.

We climbed still higher, to the small top deck, from where we gazed over the harbor and beyond to the blue-green, silver sparkles of the Adriatic Sea. We had reached the top of our new world. We decided to call this one the Star Deck.

Three-o'clock. Dockers straggled back from long lunchtimes. Steel cranes dangled long cables into our ship's hold. As the dock stirred awake, a long grey row of cranes leaned forward to begin their delicate up and down whirring and loading into the row of freighters anchored along our dock.

"They look like Trojan horses nibbling spaghetti," Alex said.

We stayed on to watch the bustle. More sailors came up onto the stern deck and expertly began pushing and packing one hold with large hessian bags of cocoa, marked for delivery to Malaysia; the other hold was tightly closed, ready to be packed once we reached Port Said with bales of cotton destined for Hong Kong. Rays from the low autumn sun washed everything into color: green, purple, and yellow for the dockers' shirts, the sugar white of the ship, brilliant blue for the wide arc of the Adriatic Sea, a delicious chocolate color for the heavy hessian bags. The two ink-black squares of the holds added emphasis.

Alex went below to unpack manuscript and toothbrush. The children and I stayed on, enthralled.

A little later we heard behind us: "Well, hi there."

We turned. A frail-looking woman hurried along the deck towards us. Hobbled by inches-high gold sandals, she wore a lime-green pantsuit with a white chiffon scarf around her neck. Her scarlet lips resembled a wound in a leathery, freckled face made all the more startling by wiry hair dyed metallic orange. Gnarled fingers twirled a long gold chain around her throat.

"Hello," I greeted her.

She smiled warily at us: "I'm Arabella. I guess we're fellow passengers. You're the first I've met so far. Are these your children?

Aren't they adorable! Is your husband around? I absolutely adore other people's husbands. You feel so safe with them, don't you?"

"I'm Jane," I introduced myself when she finally took a breath. "These are our children, Jefferson and Winslow, sometimes called Jeff and Wyd. My husband, Alex, just went to our cabin."

"Left you alone up here? Men are terrible, aren't they? My husband actually died on me and I'll just never forgive him. Life doesn't seem the same without husbands, difficult as they are when they're alive. I'm from Florida. You can tell from the accent, you know. I'm a real native. You don't find many of those any more. But I really am, born and bred. Where are you from?"

"Lots of places," I said.

"A Yankee. I guessed, you know, just by looking at you. Nothing personal, you understand. But I did guess." When I didn't say anything she went on: "You're very pretty, honey. How old are you, if you don't mind my asking?"

"Thirty-seven."

She sighed deeply. "Do you know anything about Yugoslav sailors?"

"Afraid not."

Blushing slightly, she said she was going to her cabin to dress for dinner.

"I don't like to rush. It strikes me as so gauche to go to dinner in the same clothes one has been wearing all day. I'm sure you agree. Even after my husband died I ..." But then she looked confused. She gave me a parting squeeze and left.

"Are they coming with us too?" Wyd asked, pointing to an old man and woman picking their way along the dock. They both wore brown hats, and dark brown coats reaching to their ankles, with tiny black boots peaking out below. Very slowly they climbed our steep gangplank.

"Looks like it," I said.

The children turned their attention back to loading. They chattered about everything they saw. I leaned against the railing, feeling expansive. Their joy filled me with courage. No shadow crossed the sun; no unexpected chill made me shiver. All was still, beautiful, expectant. Balanced at the center of that long, warm, autumn day, no past or future hovered, only space – the vast undiscovered space of this little, wet, round globe called Earth.

3. THE JESSENICE

The Captain's Welcome

We were the first to enter the dining room when Stefan rang the gong to announce dinner. As the children skipped excitedly ahead, Alex took my free hand and squeezed it tensely. "Don't worry," he whispered, perhaps to reassure me. "I can get along anywhere as long as I have money."

I felt perversely cheered.

Each of the four tables was invitingly set with white linen tablecloths, centered on which were platters of ruby-red pickled peppers. We chose the table farthest from the entrance, by the window. We had all showered and changed and felt festive. Alex looked splendid in hunter green corduroy trousers with an open hand-woven, yellow cotton shirt. He was a big handsome man, still in good shape at forty-three. Some grey had begun to thread his red hair, but his beard was as bushy and as vibrant as always. His eyes were green-grey and merry, although sometimes they seemed to be scanning his own private screen inside his large head. His wide, freckled face usually had a smile.

In a light-purple Greek hand-woven pantsuit and leather sandals, I was ready to run and roughhouse with the kids and yet feel presentable for our first evening aboard.

Stefan greeted us ceremoniously and served us a thick zucchini soup from a large earthenware bowl. From our table we had a theatrical view of anyone entering or exiting. We also had a splendid view of the ship's stern, the loading cranes, and the mysterious cargo holds.

As we ate the delicious soup, the dining room door opened and a new couple paused on the threshold. Resplendent in a stunning turtleneck sweater of knitted pink silk over tight black trousers, the tall, well-muscled man grinned expansively.

"I am Bjorn Andersson," he said, coming over to introduce himself and shake hands. "*Oui*, I am in manu-are – and I know all about it. Manu-are. My health, it suffered, and I am taking a rest. I am Danish. This is my wife Grace."

He waved vaguely toward the door. Grace, too, was tall and even more solidly built than Bjorn. Her hair was blond, lightly curled about a large, square, freckled face. She waited, wearing a vacant expression, in a long, white evening gown, with a well-tailored white jacket detailed in white sequins. A large, white Italian silk scarf was casually knotted around her plump neck.

Bjorn kept his back to his wife as he chattered on. She waited where she was.

"You understand I am an expert in manu-are. But I put all my money in jewels. Look! Those are all real." He turned, pointing dramatically at his wife. A string of pearls hung to her waist. Earlobes dripped large diamonds and each ring finger sparkled with massive, elegantly cut jewels. He looked back at us, his round, moist brown eyes shining: "You can tell they are real, *non*?"

Bjorn chose the table neighboring ours, then beckoned his wife. Grace walked casually over to it and slid gracefully onto her chair.

Despite her languid appearance, she held tightly to the table, her knuckles white, while Bjorn leaned expansively back in his chair. "What are you in? Not manure, I am sure," he said to Alex.

"No," Alex said, laughing. "I'm a writer."

"Sometimes it is the same thing, do you not think? You will find sensational stories to write about on this boat, *non*?" Alex smiled, a little too enigmatically I thought, since he had never written any "sensational journalism," and his silence might give Bjorn the wrong idea.

Bjorn ruffled his black curls. As Stefan served the soup, he turned to Grace and they chatted quietly in Danish. Grace seemed to relax. "Ah ha!" he barked suddenly. The children jumped. Grace tensed. "New passengers."

Two newcomers hesitated in the doorway, trying to decide on their table. They were the small, elderly couple we had watched slowly boarding earlier. Without looking at any of us, they chose the table farthest from ours. Before sitting down, they bowed formally and silently to the room.

Almost immediately afterwards, two more passengers made their appearance, waiting diffidently in the doorway for Stefan to show them to the remaining free table.

Bjorn introduced himself with a flourish.

"Harold and Bertha Clements," the man responded glumly, sounding like the new boy at school. He was about sixty, short, packed like a bag of sand. A few thin strands of iron-gray hair were placed strategically over his bald head. His grey suit and tie were carefully ironed. Bertha was spongy and poke-able, mousy hair escaping in curls around her soft neck, while her tiny eyes gleamed in a fat, florid face. Grains of perspiration trickled down her temples. A red blouse tucked into a long black wool skirt accented her pudgy form. She slightly tipped forward, then chuckled, gesturing with a small glass:

"I like a tote o' rum before dinner, don't you?"

Stefan blinked, then escorted them to the empty table.

"Yo ho ho. Rum will make you fat," Bjorn wagged a finger at her as he watched them sit down. "I never drink rum because then I do not fit into my bikini."

Bertha giggled. "You just come to me, love, whenever you 'ave a struggle. I'll 'elp you shove 'em..." her voice trailed off as she saw the children.

I introduced the four of us.

Arabella, the Floridian we'd met earlier on the deck, entered last. She posed at the door, surveying the tables. "My, we're finally all here." She waved to the room. "I'm Arabella Simpson, from Florida. Where are y'all from?" She assessed her options, and opted for the Clements' table. Her red taffeta evening gown rustled as she settled down.

Harold stated flatly that he was from Manchester, an industrial city in central England.

"What do you do?" Bjorn asked him.

"I am a goldsmith. I make medals." Harold spoke so we could all hear.

"A romantic trade," I said. "Do you make those molded chalices for churches?"

"No. Just medals."

"Do you design jewelry?" Anderson probed further.

"Money's in the medals," Harold replied. He lifted his wine glass in salute: "Bless ye all. We'll soon be on our way. May the bottom be a mile down."

"You appreciate my wife's jewels then," grinned the Dane, after the toast had been acknowledged by all but Bertha who stared pensively at the table. Harold patted her hand.

"You and my wife must have long talks some day," Bjorn turned to Arabella when Harold was silent. "You both love jewelry, I see this, *oui*."

"Oh, my goodness, yes," Arabella chirped. "My husband left me these garnets when he died. I do think that was the least he could do, don't you? I mean, after depriving me of his pension and all." The necklace was gorgeous, several strands of beads of a deep red color which hung down to her waist.

Stefan brought baskets of warm, fresh bread, cut thickly.

"*Oui*. A goldsmith. That is interesting, is it not, my dear?" Bjorn looked at his wife for approval. "There are only two kinds of crooks in the world, I think."

"And what are they, dear?" Grace asked sweetly.

Bjorn turned to his audience. "Writers and goldsmiths."

In one movement he rose to his feet, gave an entirely unexpected pirouette, then tiptoed out the room. A quiet voice spoke into the stunned silence.

"My husband is very sick. He had cancer some time ago and they took a tumor out of his brain. A silver plate covers the spot now." Grace tapped the center of her forehead. "The tumor is growing again. If anyone were to hit my husband he would die instantly."

"Good lord!" Harold said.

"My gracious," echoed Arabella. "I never would have guessed, honey. I mean, he's so *well* looking, you know what I mean? He doesn't look like a sick person. He's so tan. I always think that with a good, healthy-looking tan you just don't look sick."

The tiny, elderly couple went on eating in silence, completely ignoring the rest of us.

Grace turned to me. "I wonder if your children should not put on jackets. I was a nurse before I met my husband, so I know. Children always have some dreadful disease – measles or colds or something. I do think the captain should have warned us there would be children on board."

I could feel the mother-tiger in me rising, but then Bjorn reappeared and elegantly slid back into his place. We all watched, fascinated.

"I am told we will be loading explosives," he said, munching on a pickled red pepper.

"Oh, that can't be true!" Arabella protested indignantly.

"It's against the law with passengers on board," Alex pointed out.

"In any case, our captain would not allow it," Harold said huffily, as if he personally knew the captain.

Bertha took another sip of rum, winking at Bjorn. "You 'ave a very wicked imagination."

"In any case," Harold said, "No one can go through the Suez with explosives as cargo. And they wouldn't let us bunker in Aden either. It's one big oil tank. We could blow it and us to kingdom-come."

The Dane grinned at the commotion he had caused, then grandly turned the conversation: "I do not know much about boats, but this I know: that is the stern." He pointed forward dramatically.

His wife laughed. "No, my dear," she said. "That we call the bow. This is the stern." She patted her well-corseted bottom. Bjorn dropped his smile; Grace cringed before his stare.

"Go to your cabin," he ordered. "You shall have no dinner tonight."

We all watched her rise heavily to her feet, her wide shoulders and thick arms bulging her white jacket. The door sighed as it closed behind her.

"*Non,*" the Dane smiled at each of us in turn. "I do not want her to get fat like her mother. Her mother get so fat she split up the sides."

Alex raised his eyebrows at me and we turned our attention to the children, finishing delicious breaded veal cutlets and baked potatoes. Stefan cleared the dishes for dessert: a sweet smelling deep-dish apple pie with warm cream sauce. We kept our conversation to our table.

We were putting our napkins in their identifying rings when two giant sailors pushed open the door then stood aside, waiting in silence, muscles rippling their black T-shirts. Our captain entered and the two giant sailors smoothly fell in behind him, dwarfing his compact figure completely. We had not seen him before this. He was short and wiry, with a long face of the sort more often found on tall, bony people. Forehead and chin both came to something of a point. Cold grey eyes glittered without expression. His formal black uniform was new and stiff. He kept on his hat.

"Welcome aboard," he said grimly, walking briskly by each table, the two sailors only one step behind him. "I am Captain Stanislav. I take you to Japan and back to Rijecka. You are my cargo. You follow my orders at all times. Good night."

Arabella stood up hastily, grasping her beaded-purse in one thin hand, and holding out the other to the captain.

"How do you do?" she giggled. "I'm just thrilled to be on board your ship."

Captain Stanislav looked at her and he looked at her hand, then without a word he tacked around both and bailed. Like clockwork, the two sailors closed in behind him.

Red-faced, Arabella sat down.

All the passengers were disappointed. We had hoped the captain would preside at a table, choosing different guests each meal.

He chose instead to eat in his own dining room.

We had hoped to be asked by him to the bridge, to be shown the radar, and told interesting bits of sea lore and thrilling personal adventures over a good glass of slivovic.

The slivovic was there, no doubt about that.

But the captain? Never.

4. DALMATION COAST

We Leave

The ship set sail in mid-afternoon the following day. The children were ecstatic. This was the real beginning of the adventure. Jessenice circled just inside Rijecka harbor, checking the gyroscope, I guessed. I'd never seen a ship do this before, just make perfect circles, large and small. After an hour, we were off, sailing down the rocky Dalmatian Coast. Jeff and Wyd settled down to some serious wave watching, lying down on the passenger deck to trace the patterns resolving themselves against the side. The sea was calm. Our ship cut through the water like a knife through soft butter.

I leaned against the railing at the back of the passengers' deck and watched the desultory efforts made by five sailors to sweep and tidy around the holds. Our next unloading of cargo would be at Port Said.

Alex joined me at the railing, distracting me with a hug and a kiss.

"Whooo!" He let out a deep breath.

"What have you been up to?" I asked.

"I've been reading Jung again."

"He always makes me feel I'm bumping my head on the ceiling."

"Well, that's one way of looking at him."

"I mean he makes me feel as if the top of my head were made of cement."

"I understood."

"You didn't sound as if you understood."

"How did I sound?"

"Oh, forget it. Let's get back to Jung. What did he tell you?"

"His idea that women have a male animus, and men have a female anima, helps explain what happens when people get old and let their guard down. The men become like women, and he thinks the women become more like men."

"You knew that already. Still, I can see myself as a crusty-brained old man, can't you? And it beats being a slovenly-hearted old woman, I feel."

"Well," he said, sounding unnecessarily patient, "as women get clearer about the world, men get a richer soul life."

"Crusty has a nice delicious sound to it," I mused. "Crusty as a warm, deep-dish apple pie, with Devonshire cream."

"That's true. The crusty old mystic-sociologist Gurdjieff decided we had three brains, not only one or two."

"And King Arthur thought the brain was in the heart. He tried to make it less slovenly."

We thought about it all for a while.

"The brain in the front of the head that we have today is a fairly new invention." I said. "Probably came on about the time of Buddha."

"I think you'll find it goes further back."

"Not the one we have today: all intelligence and no warm thought. It makes for what Americans call: problems. Like 'I have a problem, he doesn't love me.'"

"You're tough. And I do love you," Alex laughed.

We were sorry to hear Arabella's spiky high heels approaching. She clutched a fluffy wool wrap around her shoulders.

"Getting some air?" she asked. "It's very chilly."

"It is damp. But the air is nice and fresh."

We'd put on thick jackets. Arabella squeezed in between us and we reluctantly moved apart. She gazed confidingly at Alex. "What did you make of that talk at dinner last night?"

"Bjorn, you mean?"

"Yes. I guess he's a pretty sick man, wouldn't you say?"

My concern for the children surfaced. "Do you think he's dangerous?"

"Oh, good gracious, do you think so too?" She touched my arm. "I do feel so awfully alone at times."

"I think we'll be okay," Alex said, stretching.

"You're wonderful, but I don't know how you can be so sure," she said. "What's Bjorn's story? Do you have any ideas?"

"Stefan told me Bjorn was in the U.N. Agricultural Division," Alex said. "Manure was his specialty."

I wrinkled my nose. "Specialty?"

"He was involved in the development of a fly-killing additive to put into manure. Apparently it's quite a problem – flies that breed in manure. His was a rather important department, I gather."

"That was before his illness?" I asked.

"Yes."

"I wonder why Grace made sure everyone knew about the plate in his forehead," Arabella said.

"She probably guessed Bjorn would drive us nuts, and wanted to warn us in case we felt like slugging him," Alex replied.

"Or maybe he's driving her nuts and she's hoping one of us will slug him," I suggested, smiling at Alex over the top of her head.

"It must be an awful thing to live with," Arabella reproved me.

"For us or for him?" Alex said.

I couldn't help laughing out loud, then turned conciliatorily to Arabella. "The freighter is a lot grander than I expected," I remarked. "I thought we'd be on a dirty, black little boat, covered with grease and ropes and shouting sailors."

"Yes, the crew might all be mutes, for all we know," she said.

"They haven't even said 'hello' to the children. But their eyes are kind, and I like all that gold in their teeth when they smile."

"It's nice they keep the ship so clean. I don't like things to be dirty." She squirmed delicately.

We made room for the Clements as they sauntered over to join us. Harold chewed on the end of his cigar.

"Horribly damp, isn't it?" he announced.

"Oh, it is," Arabella agreed. "I was just thinking to myself that I'm not one for cold weather. I'm from Florida, you know. There's something so depressing about the weather when it's cold and grey, isn't there?"

"There certainly is," agreed Bertha. "I was just tellin' 'Arry 'ow depressing it is. I keep thinking of our garden back 'ome. It's time to plant the spring bulbs."

"Bertha keeps a fine garden," Harold said.

Bertha's beady eyes focused disconcertingly on me. "My son Alfie loves my garden. He's a whiz at pruning the 'edges. One year he cut the 'edge so that it looked like a barracks. 'Arry was tickled pink, weren't you, 'Arry?"

Harold stiffened, but he was looking at something behind me. I swung around, nervously.

Bjorn.

"Do you know what the third mate tells me?" he whispered loudly.

"No," Harold said shortly, already displaying a firm dislike for the Dane.

"We are the only passengers on board until Karachi. We are stuck with only each other."

We responded with uncomfortable silence.

"Who's joining us in Karachi?" I asked finally.

"Some rich Australians. A family."

"Oh, good. Maybe children around our kids' ages?"

Harold grunted and tossed his half-smoked cigar into the dark water.

"There is more the third mate tells me." Bjorn saved his best for last. "He says we all have round trip tickets. Round-trip tickets! *Oui!* All of us. That means we will be together for the next seven months." He chortled as if he had arranged it himself, and then disappeared back down the stairs.

25

"Well now," said Harold into the silence that followed. We all looked at him expectantly, waiting as he lit a cigar and puffed complacently two slow times: "As the giraffe said when it stoock oop its head: it's all verry interesting."

* * *

We were preparing to disperse to our cabins when we realized that the ship was already turning towards shore. Daylight was fading, and it was only five o'clock. We had left Rijecka Harbor only an hour and a half earlier.

There were no lights along the coast that we could see. Curious, and slightly uneasy, we stayed together on deck, wondering why the ship was headed landwards. Suddenly, from under an evening band of clouds, the last dark red rays of afternoon sun spotlit an enormous natural wall of barren rock. It was shaped like a gigantic football stadium with water for playing field and one end blown away. Near the entrance to this inlet was an empty quay with two loading cranes. At the far end was a tiny village, its red tile roofs shining in the purple-red rays of the fast setting sun.

Stefan passed, looking anxious. I called out: "Is this our first stop?"

He glanced over his shoulder. "Yes. Captain say all passengers must go ashore right away."

The children sensed our preoccupation with the unexpected detour and were bursting with excitement while the ship moored. The gangplank was almost immediately lowered.

"Come on, kids," I said. "Let's get warmly dressed and explore the town."

Alex, who likes to take his time examining a situation, was puzzled by the captain's insistence that we go ashore immediately. So were Harold and Bertha, who met us at the top of the gangplank.

"It looks like the orders have started already," said Harold.

"Can we go with you?" Bertha asked nervously.

"Better get something warm to wear," I suggested. "Nights can get chilly if we have to stay a while. We'll walk ahead slowly. You'll catch up."

Sailors were busy opening the two back holds. None of them spoke to us. On the dock we saw stacks of crates covered with green tarpaulin. The two cranes were already in place but, as long as passengers were on board, they waited motionless to begin their mysterious meals.

The road to town was littered with debris, pieces of wood, large stones and oddly strewn bricks, rusted iron, and fallen telephone poles. It seemed to be an abandoned harbor. Bertha and Harold caught up with us as we walked slowly and carefully through the debris. We didn't want to go too far, because soon it would be night.

Before long, Arabella and the Anderssons joined us in the tiny town. It was built up the side of rocky cliffs. Cobbled stones and red tile roofs made cubist patterns of red and grey. Although windows and sometimes doors were open, the houses gave no sign of anyone inside. No one poked a curious head out to watch us go by. No one stood idly in a doorway as we were used to seeing in Greece. The pristine streets were deserted. The one hotel had its door padlocked.

We could not account for the emptiness or the silence. It was as though the entire village had been sent away for the afternoon. At the little cafe on the square only two men were seated. One of them turned away as we approached, but the waiter stood his ground and served us in stony silence.

Noticing our small, elderly passengers sitting rigidly on a small bench at the far end of the square, we waved. They did not appear to see.

"Where is everybody?" Jeff wondered as we arranged three little iron tables.

"I tell you, we load ammunition," Bjorn said, gloomily.

Dismissing his nonsense, we waited in deepening shadow for a message from the captain that we could return to the ship. An hour passed. Dusk fell but no streetlights were turned on. No villagers returned. The cafe owner brought us a short candle set deep in a green glass. We asked for something to eat or drink. He brought us slivovic and fresh bread. He grumped when some of us, particularly the kids, preferred water or coffee.

When finally our sailor-messenger arrived, the evening was deeply dark. Using a dim flashlight, he led us as fast as we could manage, single-file, back to the dock. I stayed right with him, and the kids and Alex stayed with me. We kept reminding him to wait for the others. All the lights, aboard and ashore, were off, except for one soft glow on the gangplank. In the damp air, our ship was in a cocoon of whiteness, a ghost ship in the deserted harbor.

Loading had been completed, and the holds were shut tight. No one seemed to be either ashore or aboard. Only Stefan, who waited at the top of the gangplank in his black and white clothes, creating an eerie effect since we could not make out the dark parts of him. When we reached the bottom of the stairs, he turned on a brighter flashlight to help guide us.

Once all were carefully counted as being aboard, the anchors noisily crashed on the deck.

The ship pulled away from shore as I put the kids to bed with a story and a hug. Then I went into my own cabin. It was eleven o'clock. Alex was reading on his bunk. Feeling restless, I went back to check on the children. They were already asleep. Only dim red lights lit inside corridors. Exploring further I went out on deck, standing near our cabin porthole. The ship threaded its way slowly through the myriad islands off the treacherous Dalmatian coast. Some were much too close for comfort. But it was incredibly beautiful.

I knocked on the porthole. Alex opened it.

"It's unbelievable," I said. "Come join me."

Gingerly, we climbed to the bridge where, in a sudden backlit flash from a lighthouse, we could see the captain and five officers in the wheelhouse. We sailed in total dark. As our eyes got used to it, we watched the black thickness of land outline itself against the transparent blackness of sky. Our watery passageway was sometimes so narrow I could have leaned over and touched the stony cliffs with my hand. Occasionally beacons shone forward from inky outposts on either side, narrowing together then widening as if filmed in slow motion. As we passed, they were instantly turned off.

An icy voice froze us to the deck. A flashlight blinded us.

"What are you doing here?" It was Captain Stanislav. He came right up to us, his shoulders stiff with fury.

We backed away, astonished.

"Never come here again!" his voice was loud, laced with hysteria. He kept his chin five inches from Alex's. "Never, you understand! Never anywhere near the bridge! Any of you!"

Shaking, too shocked to respond, we climbed back down to our cabins and stopped to check that all was well with the children. They still were sleeping soundly. Alex went to our cabin, but I stood between their beds for some time watching them, getting calm. They were both on their backs, arms flung out as if flying in some wonderful other world. I took comfort from their regular breathing, their soft, pink cheeks, their relaxed faces. They seemed to know their way to this other world which I, although blind to it, could sense, at least something of the courage it gave, its wealth of good feeling. I stayed until I shared some of their peace, then left them playing in their angelic place.

" He should have told us," I said to Alex, joining him in our cabin. "I always go up to the bridge. Do you think it means we are carrying something dangerous as Bjorn says, or just that we should have known better? I suppose he could have mistaken our heads for rocks."

"We probably should have known not to go to the bridge without an invitation." Alex said, putting down his book and moving over on the bunk so we could lie together. "Even so," he added as comfort, "he over-reacted. We couldn't have made him all that nervous. He's done this coast a thousand times."

He turned off the light. Soon I heard his sleep-steady breathing. I went back to my bunk under the porthole. The faint, regular beat of one diesel engine distorted the slightly irregular rhythms of my heart. Water plashed quietly outside the ship's steel wall by my pillow. Occasional footsteps passed stealthily down the long corridor. Otherwise there was silence. The ghostly ship slowly slipped along its sepulchral path, night muffling its passing.

I had been prepared for adventure when I was young, crossing the ocean with my mother, father, sister, and brother, sailing to Europe by transatlantic steamer when I was three. For the next five years, we lived in a tiny Catalan fishing village (two hours from Barcelona in our second-hand 'open' Lancia). We stayed there mostly on the golden beach for five years in the 1930's, through two mini-revolutions, until the Spanish Civil War expanded out of control.

Our friends the villagers kept us up on the intricacies of survival. Such as: when walking never appear to be carrying anything.

Don't hurry as if you were escaping someone, or meeting someone else. If you were unsure of a stranger, a brief eye contact might save your life. But use your sense, because another time it would be safer to look vague and away.

Never carry anything for anyone else.

One day a friend invited us to watch as she and some others burned down the local church. I tried out my new survival information by snatching the halo of the Madonna when it toppled off her head and rolled right towards me as she fell engulfed in flames. I kept my eyes vague and averted from the soldiers who were keeping people away at gunpoint. I was nine years old. The villagers let out one terrible groan and knelt to cross themselves. So did the soldiers. Later, as we all dispersed to our homes, I carried the cooling bronze halo safely in my hand. As we passed our friend's ground floor room, she opened the door and pointed for us to look inside. There by her bed was an exquisite picture of the Madonna that she had saved, votive candle flaming still.

In our tiny town were anarchists, monarchists, republicans, factory owners and factory hands, aristocrats, priests, students, teachers, and us. As the revolution heated up, a British destroyer was dispatched to rescue our family. We were given the captain's office that night, and I slept on the captain's desk.

After a steamer trip to the United States, and then another back over to Europe, I spent my teenage years in Italy, and stayed in Florence for the first two years of World War II until America seemed about to enter the catastrophe. Once again we escaped, boarding the last passenger ship out from Portugal. Our foreign friends who remained behind went to Italian concentration camps.

It had been a tumultuous childhood. I sighed, feeling conflicted, but safe now. There was no danger, no war. I felt responsible for the children, and certainly did not want to put them at any risk. But I liked adventure. There was already something appealing about our slightly sinister white vessel. My curiosity was roused. I knew Alex's was, too. This was partly because of our background as journalists, partly because life becomes more immediate in adventure. It always feels good to feel alive.

I sat in a balloon of darkness as the ship cut through its own larger black. I stayed awake until the motors thumped into full speed and I could feel the rocking of the open sea.

5. IONIAN SEA

We Write Our Own Stories

The ship left the gloomy Adriatic behind. The crystalline Ionian Sea cradled our snowy vessel. October turned into the mild, salty season for which there is no name on a boat. Jeff, Wyd, and I began regular morning lessons in the children's cabin. First we re-arranged the room to suit our needs. The bureau stayed between the two beds, readily accepting piles of books. Beside the reading books, there were notebooks for crayoning and painting, plus math notebooks, and poetry ones, which we had made ourselves. Scissors, paste, paper, crayons, clay, colored wool, and crocheting needles went into the two top desk drawers opposite the bureau. In one drawer we put our simple wind instruments: recorders. Boxes of toys were stored under the beds. The couch we left under the porthole so we all could easily watch the floating world. The armchair remained in the corner, ready to welcome Alex or other visitors.

The children had hung the last of their clothes in the large closet in the entrance hall. Everything was immaculately clean, highly polished or freshly painted. We stood together, arms entwined, and examined our new home with delight.

"We've really set out on quite an adventure," I said. "How would you each like to write a book about our journey as we go along?"

The kids were excited, but there was one obstacle that Wyd pointed out. "I don't know how to write."

"That doesn't matter, Wyd. You know lots, and you'll learn the rest as you go along. You tell me what you want to write about. I'll help you spell."

From the trunk I dug out two large notebooks we had bought in Athens.

"Look. Real books for you to write in. You can each use one. We'll also put in everything you find on the trip."

"Everything flat, you mean," Jeff said.

"Right. Like the leaves you found in Belgrade."

"And post cards?" Jeff was getting the idea.

"Drawings?" Wyd asked.

"Yes, and pretty cutouts, or funny things you make."

"Money?"

"Yes, and stamps, too, from all the countries we go to. And menus and matchboxes. It will be beautiful."

They were delighted with the prospect. They lugged the heavy books to their beds and opened them.

Of all the things that the children did on that trip, one of the most wonderful was writing those books. Over the course of the long journey, they would cover them with gay Japanese paper, fill them with post cards and drawings of mysterious temples, busy harbors, and strange cities, of stamps, chopsticks, hell money, menus from exotic lands, tickets for odd events, schedules in strange tongues, and even a plate made of lotus leaves sewn with palm tree fiber.

Jeff and Wyd already knew the alphabet and they had begun to build word structures. They had learned by writing letters when they lived abroad, rather than by spelling lists. It had been incentive to keep up with friends and family back in the States. There was reason to write. Furthermore, they'd get answers, too, which would inspire them to try to read.

Now I decided to use the same process in these books. They would tell me what they wanted to write. If it were needed, I would help them shorten the wording so as not to make it too onerous a task. Sometimes I would dictate to expand their oral connection with the written word; sometimes I sat back and let them ask for spelling help. After it was written they would read it out loud, from memory really, learning as they read to recognize the bunches of letters. Each day they would start by reading the entire manuscript over from the beginning. Daily new words sank into their ever-enlarging vocabulary, words for which each child had an affinity.

Words like 'but' and 'the', having no emotional hooks, could easily get mixed up. Lljubljana never did. Lljubljana was a castle town atop a small mountain in Yugoslavia. We had stayed in a hotel nearby on our way from Belgrade to Rijecka. Lljubljana Fortress consisted of massive walls that were divided into apartments and inhabited. These protective defenses guarded not the usual castle, which in this case was itself part of the thick walls, but simply an open courtyard. There was only one entrance through an iron gate. The windows had sheltered archers, but now they sprouted bottles of milk and bits of butter and shiny vegetables. Children, dressed in colored tights and short skirts or pants, played like the ghosts of Renaissance pages on crenellated fortress tops. Instead of many-colored flags, many colored clothes waved proudly, drying in the sunlight from the forbidding battlements.

Lljubljana is the way children like to spell.

Each child drew on different words, growing their verbal nature from the ground of different responses to the same experiences. Discovering new words, they passed them back and forth to each other. Their sympathy lent interest to each other's work. Like seeds in well-turned soil, a word from one child fell into the other without resistance.

I watched the mysterious process with wonder. Did the words pick the child or did the child pick the words? It was an uncanny process. Words were like soft mollusks in underwater depths, growing

invisible tentacles of discriminating consciousness to put out into
unknown currents.

* * *

After a while the children went to find Alex and pull him out on
deck. I stayed behind, lying on the couch, hands clasped behind my
head. I was counting on the process of educating the children being a
way of educating myself as well, although educating wasn't the right
word because it usually meant something coming from the outside
and then being remembered. It relegated wondrous facts to mere
measurements, formulas, and dates. It demanded a limited objectivity
and a brain without that warm elusive quality that I sought in
educating through experience.

Without warning, Bjorn's tanned, round head grinned down at me,
framed by the porthole. It was a perfect fit. I was dismayed to find
that the portholes opened onto the passenger deck just at Danish head
level.

"Do you know why the crew are not permitted to converse with
us?"

"I hoped it was a language difficulty," I said unenthusiastically.

"My friend the third mate tells me anything I wish to know. He
has been forbidden to speak to me. He tells me the crew has been
given orders not to fraternize with the passengers. Not even with the
children."

"Why not?"

"Because we're from capitalist countries. Theirs is a communist
one. They may speak only to Herr Doktor and Frau Doktor because
they come from Dresden, which, as you know, is in East Germany,
and Communist. I am a man of the world, so I understand their point
of view. You also. You are like me, *non*?"

Like a cork being pulled, Bjorn popped his grinning head out of
sight.

I am not like him at all, I told myself definitely. I could not
understand the captain's order. I did not believe that people, when
one-on-one, really acted politically. Within the framework of

individual encounter, most people could be counted on to be friendly and trustworthy. It was only under the coercion of ideology that humans murdered and warred.

I sighed. Part of the adventure of a freighter trip was the camaraderie between passengers and crew. You're all in the same boat, so to speak, and for a moment there is a truce, a bit of brotherhood. I had counted on magical excursions to the inferno of motors or to the treasure trove of holds and galleys to create for the kids an aura of friendliness and kindness in a very big world, a bumper of trust put out to an otherwise unfamiliar situation. Why forbid a friendly word between children and crew? What danger could they present?

The cabin door crashed open and the children entered, loudly banging the dinner gong, their faces shining.

"Stefan said we could ring the gong for meals!" Jeff grinned.

"We go along all corridors and once around the deck upstairs!" Wyd added.

I cheered up. "Lunch time already?"

"Yes! Stefan said twelve o'clock," Jeff called over his shoulder, pulling Wyd out into the corridor. "Come on!"

The children danced out and around the surging ship.

* * *

"Do you want to hear what I've figured about Grace and Bjorn?" I asked after the kids were asleep and Alex returned fresh and cool from a solitary moonlit stroll on deck. I was already in his bunk.

"I want to," he said as he began to undress.

"Well, I think what they both say, which is different from each other, is all true. But it needs a twist. I think that Bjorn was very sick, and slightly askew."

"That's established." Naked, he rolled onto the bunk with me.

"So, lots of nurses not only swab and feed and inject their charges, but take 'caring' to more exciting levels. You know what I mean. They're tender, speak lovingly, entice, arouse, and satisfy their charges. They withhold or give as they choose. Maybe Grace got him hooked on something and now successfully controls his suffering in some way. They get married, leave the hospital, and live ever after."

"Happily ever after?"

"No, Just 'ever after.'"

"Good God!" Alex turned off the light and we kissed. "What an imagination."

6. MEDITERRANEAN SEA

Puppet Show

A week of fresh warm breezes, the idle round of mid-sea travel, and the regularity of morning classes combined to shed the clouds of unease that had gathered around the ship.

With all of Greece and its islands now floating by to the north of us, I told the children the Aesop's Fables which had originated there. To tell the ancient tales, we used unusual handmade Hungarian puppets. These brought the morality fables to life and added fun to the telling. After a while the children could repeat the stories to each other using the puppets themselves. As I spread them out on the bed one morning, ready for the next lesson, Wyd asked:

"Mum, can we give a puppet show?"

"Oh, yes!" Jeff put in eagerly. "We know lots of stories now. Can we?"

"For all the passengers?" Wyd asked.

"All the passengers and Stefan?" Jeff added.

"Sounds like a great idea," I said, bravely.

"First we have to make a program," Jeff planned.

"And tickets," Wyd interrupted, looking around for scissors and paper.

"How much should we charge?" Jeff asked.

"One dinar should do it," I said. Even that might cause dissension, but figuring seven hundred and fifty to the dollar, it would cause the least dissension possible.

Jeff was satisfied. He did not yet know the buying power of one dinar.

The first part of the morning passed choosing fables from those the children already knew. Jeff wrote the titles. Wyd busied herself with tickets and programs. When all was ready, they asked Stefan if they could post arrows in the corridors to direct passengers to the theater in their cabin, and with his permission also pinned an elaborately decorated program in the lounge. The show would take place in the children's cabin before lunch.

When I walked down the corridor a while later the arrows had disappeared.

"Yes, Frau Doktor Rikstoffer pointed them out to me," Stefan said apologetically. "I did not think them a mess, but she say she notify captain."

I returned to the cabin.

"Let's include *Dog in the Manger*," I said. "Read the program, Jeff."

"*Little by Little Does the Trick*. Actor: Crow."

Wyd picked up the black crow dressed in a patchwork suit. It could take up nuts in its beak and fill a jar, if done little by little, as told in the story.

Goose and the Golden Egg. Actor: Chicken.

Wolf in Sheep's Clothing. Actors: Fox and Lamb.

Dog in the Manger. Actor: Shaggy Dog.

Promptly at eleven-thirty, the audience began to arrive. Grace seated herself elegantly in the only armchair. Bertha and Harold on straight-backed chairs. The almost-silent Rikstoffers meekly sat back against pillows on the bunk across from the stage. Stefan leaned against the door, a large green feather duster hanging from his back pocket, eyes alert to possible interruption from the corridor. Bjorn stood with him in the doorway. Arabella had not yet arrived. Alex stood near the stage in case of catastrophe. He remembered vividly how, playing Herakles with a large club, he had brought down the whole set when he was eight years old, A sheet-draped armchair served as puppet stage. Kneeling on their bunk, concealed behind another armchair, the children worked the hand puppets.

The Shaggy Dog got up from his bed to tell the tale and firmly point its moral:

"People often begrudge others what they cannot enjoy themselves."

"That is a story we tell in Denmark," Bjorn announced in surprise. "This is interesting, Jane. These stories are like you and me, they are international."

Stefan smiled his gentle smile: "I too hear that story as a boy."

"*Wolf in Sheep's Clothing*," Jeff announced. "We use Fox instead of Wolf."

"Because we don't have a wolf," Wyd popped up to explain.

Jeff pushed her down disapprovingly, and disappeared himself. Wyd's enthusiasm for the fables focused on the animals that she loved and played with as friends. Jeff's was also for the animals, but more for the moral, which came at the end of each playlet. He held up the fox we had dressed as a Wolf in Sheep's Clothing, and savored the moment:

"Appearances are deceptive."

"Aha!" Bjorn jumped in glee. "How true that is. Isn't it so, Jane?" He looked pointedly at Harold. "It is just like some people we both know. You can never tell about them. How wise the little ones are."

Harold moved to the other side of the room, away from him. "There's a lot less hot air over here," he explained blandly.

"You're doing fine, kids." Alex laughed encouragingly. "Go right ahead."

The children were oblivious.

Arabella showed up half-way through the next playlet. "Since I'm late I don't think I should have to pay," she said.

No one paid attention.

"That's all right," Harold started. "If you ask me…"

Wyd interrupted with the punch line of her story: "Familiarity Breeds Contempt."

"That one is so true," Grace murmured, loud enough to hear over the clapping.

"Maybe that's enough for today, eh, kids?" I suggested.

"But everyone's paid for their tickets!" Wyd protested. "We *have* to finish."

"Mrs. Arabella has not yet paid," Frau Doktor Rikstoffer remarked. "It's only fair to the children that she pay."

"*The Mouse and the Lion*," Jeff went on, ignoring the interruption.

Wyd was by his side, smiling broadly. Alex stood proudly, arms crossed. The story was Jeff's favorite. He was radiant as he pronounced the moral: "Little people can be big friends!"

Everyone clapped loudly and I relaxed. Jeff popped up over the hanging sheet, smiling at the loud round of applause. He pulled Wyd up for her share of the bow.

"You know," he said, incandescent, "that's true. Little people *are* big friends. Because it's not bigness like – like a ball or something. It's bigness *inside*."

7. SEA OF CRETE

Storms

I took courage from the morning's success. The children had had fun, and everyone had been cheerful and friendly at lunch. Even the Rikstoffers offered us a stiff smile when they entered the dining room. Ignoring Bjorn's discouraging gossip, I decided it was time to break the heavy ice that lay between passengers and crew. I was certain that the sailors would eventually offer to show Jeff the forbidden corners of the ship that he longed to explore, like the engine room and the radio room.

I understood his longing although I hadn't dared return to the bridge yet. Besides, the radio equipment we had glimpsed briefly upon first coming aboard seemed too sophisticated to be of much interest. The old-fashioned radar screen we'd experienced on the Greek freighter that we'd taken from New York to Piraeus, with its little blobs moving straight across a nest of circles to seek out anything in a radius of twenty miles, seemed more fun. Still, it might be good for Jeff to try to understand this more modern equipment as it acted on the very ship we sailed on. It would be a way of fusing the abstract and the experiential – the kind of thing I continually sought for the children.

Together, Jeff and I climbed to the windy top deck, keeping our eyes peeled for Savo, the radio operator. Jeff was anxious. From the top of the ladder-stairs he had watched Savo pacing outside his radio room, but Jeff had not dared approach the huge, black-eyed man. He had told me Savo reminded him of a caged tiger. I knew why: there was something about him to be deeply feared – and sorry for, too.

"There he is," Jeff said, strengthened by his morning success. "Let's ask him."

We walked slowly. I wanted to give Savo enough time to duck out of sight, as the crew usually did when any of the passengers approached. But to my surprise Savo met us half way. He patted Jeff on the head, looking distracted.

"Hello, Mrs. Eliot."

"Hello, Savo. Are you okay?" He ran his hands through already disheveled black hair. "No. My wife," he replied. "I see her only five months in two years. I not wish this trip. She is, how you say?" He outlined a fat stomach to demonstrate pregnancy.

I was sympathetic. Savo turned to Jeff. "You like to see my room?" Delighted, Jeff nodded. We followed Savo around the side of the deck. He stooped into a tiny corridor and flung open a door. Peering inside, I saw the messiest, smelliest sleeping quarters I had ever seen. Dirty clothes hung from every hang-able spot. The bed was grimy and unmade. One sneaker lay forlornly in a small, blackened, corner sink. Ashtrays were piled high with crushed butts. A full wastebasket tipped onto the stained carpet.

Savo pushed us inside the room and shut the door. Aware of Jeff's disappointment, I held his hand, not sure what to do. Savo rummaged behind a pile of dirty clothes stacked under the sink. With an air of triumph he produced an unlabelled bottle of slivovic and poured two glasses. He offered one to me with an exultant grin, and one to Jeff who, baffled, refused.

It was only then that I realized Savo was drunk. Reluctantly accepting the slivovic, I drank to his health.

"No health this trip." Gloomily Savo shook his big head, his tongue thick. "Why do you come?"

I fidgeted nervously.

"This trip very dangerous." Savo's gloom seemed to cheer him. "If they know you are Communist it not matter too much. But it be difficult to tell just by look. You walk off the big road in Vietnam and nobody ever see you again. In Indonesia they kill you soon as they understand you American. You no want to go to East. You no want to stay on boat. I no want to stay on boat. Orders only say I go."

I wasn't sure how to respond. We had heard about the unrest in Malaysia and Indonesia and there had been some reports about trouble in Vietnam, but not enough to make us anxious. If Jeff hadn't been with me I might have prodded Savo for more details.

"Will you show us your radio room, Savo?" I asked.

Savo's bloodshot eyes grew ferocious. "You are not allowed in radio room."

I inclined my head towards Jeff. Savo's sudden hostility subsided.

"You do not want to see radio room," he addressed Jeff. "There is nothing there."

"But we saw – " broke in Jeff.

"You do not want to see," Savo interrupted. "You do not want this trip." Smiling dolefully, he offered to pour another slivovic.

I hoped that I had stayed long enough to be able to leave without offending fragile Balkan sensibilities. I shook his hand and thanked him for the drink. Savo responded profusely, thanking me for coming. The conversation continued as I backed out the door: thanking him for being asked, for being asked for another time, and for the possibility of many more slivovics together.

"With your husband," Savo said, bowing gracefully to Jeff.

"But why do you suppose they'd be so strict about keeping us out of the radio room?" I asked Alex later that evening. "It's just a few steps out of the way when we go up to the Star Deck. Seems public enough."

"I can't imagine," Alex answered. "Unless Savo was too drunk to understand what it was you wanted."

"I think he was perhaps less drunk than he pretended to be. I think he was trying to warn me that all those revolutions and mini-wars going on in the east are more dangerous to us personally than they've been reported."

"Could be." Alex gazed out the porthole at the vivid sunset. "What do you think we should do?"

"What can we do?"

"We could take his advice and get off at the next port."

"At Port Said? We can't just get off because we're puzzled. We'd need a better reason. Savo didn't give me any reason at all. Besides, where would we go? Back up the pyramids?"

"I know, but – "

"Anyway, we don't have the money: we have no house to go to, air fares would use up all our spare change; we'd have to find schools, get a job, medical insurance, everything. The only thing we have is car insurance but now we have no car. As my mother used to say: 'We're all front and no rear.'"

"It's true," Alex agreed, turning from the porthole. "And at least if we stay on the boat we have enough to make side trips to some truly remarkable places, since we have no other expenses."

"Oh well," I said, hopefully, "Savo may simply have disapproved of me. It may only be a Balkan thing about women staying home with the kids. Who knows?"

"Who knows," Alex came over and gave me a reassuringly big hug. Arms around each other, we turned back to the porthole and the first stars of sunset.

* * *

The Greek Morea unfurled to port side, occasionally nudging its fragrant coast out towards Jessenice, and pulling back into heat-shimmering distance. The ship kept to its straight watery path, plowing evenly through the slight roughness.

I stood at the forward part of the cabin deck. The wind was blowing fresh, with not a trace of earth in it. I loved the scent of earth in the wind and missed it now. There is something prophetic about the freshness of a wind at sea. My earth-bound body knew it would return to dry autumn leaves, new green grass, sun-filled wild flowers. But will the rest? Will that formless motion that presses and batters like a wild wind inside someday mix with the wind or the water and take on shapes not ordered by earth? What was that wild inner churn inside me, and what would it become?

The white freighter floated past the purple rocks of barren southern Greece. I was homesick. I rarely feel that way. Sometimes I miss a person, sometimes I need something that another place offers, but I rarely experience that sickly desire to rush back to the safety of the already familiar. Nor do I look back for that sense of wonder that I feel I should unravel, as does a silkworm its threads of silk, from my own insides.

Gazing now over the dark blue sea, the color of a great Malaga grape, fresh and succulent as it stretched to the solid purple rock, so exact and unpuzzling, I longed to return to Greece. I longed to walk on the quartz-covered mountain behind our house. I longed to swim in the historic sea at Marathon, and watch the silver fish leap about the children. Our neighbor's ancient grandmother would be sitting, serene and beautiful, under the grey-green sinews of a four-hundred-year-old olive tree, listening to the chatter of tree-frogs. In the green dusk she could hardly be distinguished from its twisting strength.

My heart ached for familiar sights. The sun sinking behind the mountains would be setting evening fire to each distinct golden needle in the pine trees. I longed to sit on the hard earth and talk to Joachim about his goats. I could almost hear their bells in the distance: they would be rounding the red-earthed crest of the mountain right about now, a river of silver sounds flowing slowly down through the fragrant air.

I remembered the dew-covered wild flowers in the meadow behind the house. A field so full of flowers, how could each be named? Yet in that astoundingly clear Greek light, I had come to realize that each flower was a distinct entity and it was my own blindness that stopped my knowing each one separately. My limited life span, even. How can your mind and heart encompass a whole field of flowers, each one separately, when you still have trouble distinguishing among strangers? And yet, I had made friends.

A purple crocus grew in the marble-hard earth under the pine trees, just three inches tall, with transparent purple wings a-top a green-gold stem. He used to stand as straight as a pine tree, and catch each sunbeam in his tiny chalice. He took all he could without stretching, and let the rest spill over. Nothing more happened except that he would never let me sit out under the pines without talking to me.

I said, You are beautiful.

He said, Beauty is simply the cloak of the unfinished.

I said, But you are almost finished now. You'll be gone in a week.

He said, These pines will be gone in fifty years, and the stars in fifty billion. What is the difference?

I said, I'm not asking for a perpetual motion machine. Fifty billion years is good enough.

You do not realize, he answered, his delicate petals turning the golden sunlight purple before letting it pass on, that time is simultaneous, not a tunnel. You see billions of years in one instant when you see a star. You don't see years and years of rain and sun when you look at a pine tree – you see the whole tree, its past, its present at once. You spread me out over only a week's time, but imagine if you were able to look at the sun and spread him out over his time. He'd be just as short-lived as you think I am. Or you might be as long-lived as he. Maybe you are more than time.

The little crocus insisted on talking about things un-trivial. He talked relentlessly. He lasted longer than he should have, and came back each year. And he would come back this year, too, and I would not be there.

Bjorn Andersson flowed into my reverie. He was leaning over the railing right beside me, his arm touching my own – just enough to impose, not enough for me to take exception.

47

"It's windy here. Getting rougher. My wife gave me a sea sickness pill. If not I would be in bed vomiting all over the floor. *Oui.* I simply cannot sail in rough weather."

I glanced at the mild waves. "We're walled by the island of Crete here, so we don't get the full brunt of the current from the Bosphorus."

"Those clouds look as if they bring storms. It is the rainy season, *non?*" His orange and black shirt was unbuttoned to his waist and he toyed with the two gold chains around his neck.

I looked at the sky. Fig-purple, dusty-rose, and saffron clouds stretched peacefully – or was it violently? – across the sky. The waves seemed calm enough.

"I don't think so," I said. "Not this far south. Just evening flourishes. "

"The Clements have already retired. They are going to have dinner in their room. I ordered my wife to stay in her room also. I do not want her sick in the dining room."

"I like the waves. It's a little change. If you stay in the fresh air you don't get sick."

"I ordered her not to have dinner for this entire week. I do not want her to get fat. I tell her, look at Jane. She is not young but she is not fat."

I did not answer.

"Ah Jane, Jane. You know I can talk to you. My wife, you see, did not marry me for love. You know how to keep secrets. So I tell you. She marries me for my money. It is simple. She is a nurse. She knows the doctors say I will die and she wants my money. But then, upon meeting her, I get the will to live. I *live*. Think of that!"

"How nice," I said, unenthusiastically.

"And even if this is not true about her, how shall I ever know for sure?"

The sun had set. The sky was still brilliant but with heavier, more lurid colors. The sea turned an ominous sleek grey, not yet black.

"I just met the captain," Bjorn pressed on. "He did not speak to me. But I speak to him. I do not let him pass in the corridor. You know how narrow it is? I said 'Good evening', and it is rough weather we are having. He had to say 'Good evening'. I will not have such rudeness. I am used to politeness and I insist. But it was peculiar. Because he was in the passenger portion, outside your door. He was with the second mate. They were looking for Savo, the radio *operateur*. They are most worried. I went to find my friend the third mate. He told me what is happening. Savo is drunk. He has been forbidden to drink, so they put him in chains. So now we are out of radio contact. That is most serious, *non*?"

"There must be someone else aboard who knows how to operate a radio."

Bjorn laughed and with mock patience slowly shook his head. "No one else. We have very special equipment that only Savo knows how to use. That is why he had to come on this trip even though his wife is pregnant. You know this."

The waves moved restlessly. Anxiety prickled me. I wished Bjorn would go away before he crashed the whole inverted bowl of colored light into smithereens.

"Why did you get Savo drunk, Jane?" he asked, edging closer. "You went to his room and got him drunk. Did you learn anything of interest?" His sooty electricity crackled around us like miniature lightning.

"I wanted Jeff to see a radio room. Savo misunderstood and took us to his cabin."

"Ah, but why did you want to see the radio room?"

"Jeff was excited, naturally. I don't see why it's forbidden."

"But you are Americans. It is natural that they are suspicious, *non*?"

The waves threatened, the wind chilled. Bjorn finally sauntered off, hands in his pockets. I looked away at sea and sky: a storm of foreboding.

As the waves roughened I remembered the last time I crossed the Aegean Sea. We had sailed above the north coast of Crete that time. Alex and I were on a yacht along with two friends, executives from Time Magazine to whom the boat had been lent by the Greek president. It was springtime and the sea was rough enough. We were warned about a ferocious mid–Aegean current that runs from Thrace on the northern Greek coast, directly down to the storm-wracked north coast of Crete. At the time I did not believe in the possibility of danger, in spite of the tremendous waves battering our small boat. I had been on the Atlantic Ocean in a transatlantic liner when waves reached to seventy-four feet. Currents that had already run their course down the Aegean Sea could not frighten me.

But now, listening to Bjorn, I shivered, and went inside. Alex was lying on the kids' sofa, the two children half by his side, half on top of him, talking. Encouraged and reassured, I joined them.

Later on, after dinner, feeling heartened, restless, curious, in love, ecstatic with the wonder of the night, I went back up to the Star Deck, where I held on to the rail, as the waves dipped the boat way down and then tossed us high in the air. I laughed as the strong wind blew my hair into tangles, and salt spray made the deck slick and slippery. All the others were below. Only the captain and I were out on our separate decks.

I said to myself: "If he can be out on deck, then I can too. I am strong, like him."

I was happy. It felt good to have memories, stories to tell, events to measure myself against. As our freighter rocked to the roughness of the north wind that now roiled the sea, I finally went below. The kids were asleep. Alex was sleepy, but still waiting. Quickly I climbed in bed, ever thankful for the warmth he never failed to give me.

8. CYPRUS

Aphrodite's Pool

A day later we were well under Turkey, sailing past the island of Cyprus, which geographically is to Turkey as a baby whale is to its mother. As I stood by myself in my funnel forest, I slipped back to the day Alex and I had bathed in the Sacred Pool of Venus – the one she swims in to renew her virginity. It's located on the northern shore of Cyprus, but not on the maps, nor in the minds of antiquity officials.

You might think that spring is enough of an aphrodisiac on Aphrodite's island to do the trick on its own: curvaceous mountains beguile in their flowery dresses; little black pigs chase about the fallen columns of Aphrodite's temples; doves bill and coo on the dusty altars of the All Holy Mother of God, in tiny neglected churches whose domes bulge with life; and the lusty calls of unusually impatient donkeys fill the air. When penetrated by eager bees, red trumpet-like pomegranate blossoms tremble delicately. Booted in pollen, the busy bees also hold intercourse between yellow broom flowers and delicate white olive blossoms, making for a spicy olive oil. The fig hangs heavy on the tree.

But no.

Cypriot farmers celebrate the day Venus-Aphrodite came ashore, by taking their little black pigs to the beach, and throwing them into the sea – a violent aphrodisiac. Pigs procreate when panicked. They swim wildly to the nearest mate, find the shallows and go to. Everyone celebrates with fresh Cypriot wine and, well you get the picture. Perhaps that's why when you bathe together, you may then have to stay together?

Legend has it that Cronus, God of Time, castrated his Father, the Space God Uranus whose testicles fell into the foaming waves where – what with one thing and another – Aphrodite was born. Climbing aboard her famous half-shell, and supported by millions of transparent scallops that, luckily for her, were up and procreating at the time, she was wafted onto a moonlit beach on Cyprus. Ever since, she is said to renew her virginity once a year by swimming in these waters. It follows, with the logic of legend, not so much that you renew your virginity if you swim here, but that if, together, two lovers who bathe in her sacred pool, stay together forever.

Being skeptical by nature, Alex and I decided to give it a try. We checked into the legendary Queen Victoria Hotel with its lady-like lace doilies and white lace curtains, in Nicosia, capital of Cyprus, and joined up with Karl and Libby, two archeologist friends from Israel. Cyprus is dedicated to the female. It sunbathes in the far eastern Mediterranean, embraced, if you will, by the patriarchal countries of the Golden Crescent: Syria, Lebanon, Israel, and Egypt. Patriarchal diet dictates no shellfish or ham on the sand which is there. And guess what animal is sacred to Venus-Aphrodite? Pig, of course. Little black pigs. As we cut into our succulent ham, the best ever, before or since, the Victorian dining room filled with "enemies" from the mainland. Forbidden to meet in their homelands, or even to eat ham at all, they were patting their stomachs and negotiating business deals over the sacred local dish.

There were no official directions to the Pool of Venus, understandably, because it was not open to the public, but we were mystified by official embarrassment when we asked about it. And why was the Sacred Stone of Venus hidden in a dark corner of the Archaeological Museum? A smooth, green meteorite rock about four feet high, its base with the same measurements as its three sides, was so ancient no one dared date it, or even agree that the symmetrical object had been shaped by human hands. As we pondered, island women came into the shadows, looked around for guards, then surreptitiously rubbed themselves against it. The museum director blushed when we asked about it, but a Greek friend, Panos, took us to a remote farm, where a lively octogenarian farmer showed us yellowing photographs of large, smiling Cypriot families.

"One day, long ago, there was a great storm with loud thunder and lightning. My stone was washed down the mountains from a temple of the Goddess." He chuckled lasciviously. "When they wanted children, women came from all over the island to sit on my stone. Sometimes they came by car, but it worked better when they arrived on donkeys."

The Archbishop, however, insisted the Venus stone go to the museum.

"I warned them not to move it. Very bad luck. It tipped over and killed a man."

So much for love.

Alex, Karl, Libby, and I crisscrossed a good deal of the island in our search for the ancient tree that guards the Pool of Venus. We finally saw it: an unbelievably gigantic creature sprawled across the side of a steep hill. A lone fig tree was to ancient travelers what a McDonald's sign is to the world: food and drink – and in this case we felt sure, Sacred Pool. As old as time, the extraordinary tree had never been cut. Silvered with sweat, we stopped the car and clambered up the almost unused path. There we found the oval opening to Venus' retreat, modestly hidden behind large green fig leaves.

With trepidation, we parted the leaves and slipped inside. Almost invisible in the dim interior, a spring flowed from a mossy cleft in the naked rock into a small, shallow, oval pool rubbed smooth by the bodies of believers over thousands of years. Emboldened by tradition, Alex and I doffed our clothes and splashed down. In the warm, refulgent wetness we were brushed by tendrils of soft green moss, and caressed by the musky roots of the fig tree.

Libby refused, so Karl bathed by himself. Their affair ended three months later. Alex and I are still together and, as in any good marriage one is apt to, sometimes we credit, and sometimes we blame that hour in her Sacred Pool.

9. PORT SAÏD

Climbing Pharaoh's Tomb

We passed Cyprus without incident and bent south towards Egypt. Desert heat pressed the water to smoothness. A bronze sun turned the sky yellow and burned the passengers. We soon discovered the cool that comes from covering one's body.

Upon learning we were nearing the African continent, we woke the children early and took them on deck to catch our first glimpse of land. The morning star twinkled in the gently opalescent sky. Alex and I knew Egypt, having visited the country by boat as far up as the Aswan Dam before it was built, and it never failed to evoke something mysterious in me, something disturbing, and wonderful, too.

We were on deck to see the sun rise. It was surprisingly cool. The empty early-morning sky slowly turned dusty yellow as desert heat followed upward.

"Look!" Jeff pointed to the sea ahead.

We squinted against the rising sun. We were being escorted by a school of nineteen dolphins, swimming and leaping in blue and silver splashes around our boat. The water was deep, transparent blue.

Then in the distance the clear, sapphire Mediterranean changed to a luscious, cocoa brown. It was as if someone had drawn a fan-shaped line with no fuzzy edges anywhere.

"What is it?" Wyd asked as the boat approached the hard-edged change. At one moment we crossed from transparent, dancing blues into opaque, liquid brown.

"It's the Nile," Alex explained.

"It's a river of mud," Jeff's eyes said in awe.

Our eyes could not see even an inch through the thick mixture. The flat brown water stirred impenetrable feelings, as if we were preparing ourselves for fierce revelations hard to swallow.

Alex described the Nile to the children:

"Its head-waters are high in the south, bubbling up amid the secret Mountains of the Moon. In spring, the Nile floods, turning the desert along its banks into farmland for the summer season. Its muddy current stains the blue Mediterranean for miles and miles out, in a fan-shaped pattern. The Nile passes some of the most ancient cities in the world, and some of the most mysterious constructions ever made: the pyramids, the Sphinx, and vast underground tombs."

The most astonishing tomb that Alex and I had visited was like an enormous underground parking lot. Instead of cars, it had Cadillac-sized marble sarcophagi. Ornate marble covers, like frosting on ice cream cakes, topped each one. And there were hundreds, perhaps thousands of them, each one containing the mummified remains of a sacrificial, milk-white bull. That was the only time before or since that I experienced claustrophobia.

Seen from the hot deck the broad flow of brown thickness underneath us was unsettling. I already missed the light-hearted sparkle of the transparent blue and silver water we had just left behind. The Nile was life giving. Even generous, as the fluid settled many feet deep along its banks and sometimes as far as a mile inland.

But unlike the blue Mediterranean, it did not share the mysteries of the life of the spirit. In Egypt you are on your own for that.

Our white ship glided across what almost looked like dry sand. There, in the arid expanse, is cause and effect: the sun makes a shadow; the water brings life; the pyramids hold it all in place like giant paperweights. People struggle. Cause and effect: cause for compassion, the effect of suffering. In the desert, the freewheeling play of Greek light and Greek gods only bewilders and offends. To experience Egypt is to be born in the flesh. It is to know the dust you are made from.

The sun had lifted powerfully into the now bronze sky. As we neared land, but still far from shore, we passed hundreds of ships at anchor, spread far and wide outside the liquid mud of the harbor, waiting their turn to convoy through the famous Suez Canal – the watery path that would lead us across the desert from the Mediterranean to the Red Sea. For those heading to and from the East, it cuts out the long voyage around Africa. We watched the blue and silver dolphins ease around our knife-edged prow. They glided into the air, then back under water, in one ecstatic motion, a little like night and day, or life and death, all the while playfully escorting our ship to its berth in the northern harbor of Port Said.

Bjorn joined us. "*Non*, Alex. It cannot be the Nile. We are still much too far from shore."

"It's the Nile," Alex answered. "Or rather it's the river's afterthought."

"The Delta," I explained.

Bjorn shrugged genially. "Fortunate we are a long way from land, because our radio *operateur* is drunk again and we maneuver with hand signals. Come, children, we play tag. Jeff, you are it!" He slapped his shoulder hard and galloped off.

I winced for Jeff, but he did not seem to mind the slap. Lightly he tapped Wyd's arm.

"You're it!"

He sped after Bjorn.

The happy shouts from the children grew distant. We turned back to the railing. Even though we were to do no more than touch her lightly on this visit, it was still enough to squeeze Egypt's dusty hand in reverence.

Greece, I mused, is so different that the two countries seem thousands of miles apart. Greece ignores the sun burnt, physical side of yourself, and instead lets light enter to fill you with spirit. The past is not long ago, but right now, to be lived. Then, sometimes, you feel as if the whole sparkling top could be peeled off – green needled trees, purple mountains, silver sea, blue sky – to find the pulsing order behind its unique beauty. The Egyptian desert is different. There is responsibility in its squat, glaring-white houses, shimmering in the heat; predictability in its straight roads leading from silent towns to empty horizons. Its flat sands seem to move in tune with the silent beat in our temples. An occasional rocket-thin minaret pierces the skyline as if pinning one of the many shining domes in place.

"Are we supposed to believe that bit about hand-signals?" I asked Alex, marveling at the way our ship zipped across the increasingly crowded stretch of brown water, maneuvering through an obstacle course of vessels, as though it were a little speedboat.

"It would be pretty nervous-making if true. I doubt it. And doubt beats worry, doesn't it?"

"It's always best," I said, dissatisfied by his lack of certainty.

The children came back, breathless from chasing Bjorn around the deck, and began to try to identify the flags of the other ships – Japan, China, Russia, Italy, England, Greece, Turkey, Liberia, Panama, Venezuela. The list went on and on, including new countries we had not yet heard of. The ships came in all sizes: large snow-white passenger ships, long eerie tankers, bobbing empty for their journey through the canal, snappy freighters like ours, scruffy working vessels, and more, all the way down to hundreds of little mud-stained sailing craft for use around the delta. Over the coming months we would get to know many of the larger vessels, for they sailed the same watery way we did, meeting a similar schedule to ours.

Our ship stopped for a while, well off-shore. But by breakfast time we were moored on the Suez Canal itself, just opposite the town. We waited impatiently for the gangplank to be lowered. We were ready to get off immediately and take advantage of our short time in this exotic place. It was still early morning. We would have breakfast in town. The children hopped eagerly from foot to foot, chattering together. This was our first real stop.

Arabella joined us. She had on a brown and white sundress and gold mules.

"Aren't you going ashore?" I asked.

"Say, didn't you hear? We aren't allowed off in Port Said this morning. The captain has given orders."

"You're kidding!"

"Yes, not till this afternoon, after lunch. From three to six."

It was not yet eight o'clock. I sensed the children's disappointment and felt it keenly myself.

"That's ridiculous! The town will be closed up tight at that time of day."

"I know. And when we go, we have orders to stay together and stay with our guide the whole time. None of us are allowed off on our own. Stefan asked me to tell you."

"How do they plan to stop us?" Alex laughed. "Kidnap us in the streets?"

"We won't be allowed back on the ship unless we stick with our guide and we're on the exact same boat that takes us to shore."

We squinted across the canal at a long line of small, identical, black dhows, one of which was to take us to shore later in the day. They were more like low rectangular platforms than boats. Each was black, and each had a dark, straight-backed man in a long black robe, holding a long black oar, standing in the stern. The boats bumped gently together in the barely rippling water. There was no telling one from another.

"I've never heard anything so absurd!" Alex said. "I'll check it out with the third mate."

"Let me talk to Stefan," I offered. "He makes more sense."

I found him busy in his pantry and stopped at the door. His thin frame seemed to fill the small space. Standing where he was in the middle of the room, he could touch the refrigerator on one side and the counter space on the other without moving. Even the topmost shelves were within his long reach. In one corner there was a tall

59

stool. Stefan did not do the cooking for our meals, but in his limited space he prepared the cold appetizers, cut and toasted bread, and set out the food from the wooden dumb-waiter that was hauled up by hand from the galley two decks below. Four salt and pepper shakers, four marmalade jars, four jugs of pickled red peppers, and four sauce bottles were lined neatly on the counter. Four water jugs stood back against the counter wall. Four brown ceramic teapots squatted in front. Serving platters were stacked nearby along with breadbaskets and sugar pots. Stefan made afternoon tea and morning coffee, served wines and juices. He had already cleared away the breakfast dishes, and was setting up for lunch. The cupboards were open, displaying neatly stacked plates, cups and glasses.

"Hello, Missus." Stefan went on counting out knives and forks.

"The captain won't allow us to get off before three this afternoon."

"Yes?"

"It doesn't make any sense! It's a little like being held prisoner. The town will be closed up tight in the afternoon."

"I am sorry, but it is impossible to leave before then. We load cotton."

"So?"

"Then we move ship and stop for the afternoon, Missus." He spread his arms, his bony hands splayed. "I cannot help you before then."

"What do you mean?"

"You will be able to leave at three o'clock with the rest. I will make sure." It was a promise. He turned back to his counting.

Discouraged, I went back to Alex and the children and told them what Stefan had said.

They'd found a small piece of shade on the starboard side of the passenger deck. It wasn't long before vendors in beautiful blue and green robes clambered on board from their black dhows, and began lining the bottom deck with their crude but wonderful wares. A stately old man, wearing a long, blue silk robe, climbed up to our deck. He pulled a handful of objects from his wide sleeve.

"We are not allowed to sell these," he murmured, looking over his shoulder.

"What are they?" I asked.

"They were dug up by little boys, in my own village. Perhaps they have been under the earth for four thousand years."

The children examined a scarab the man offered. It had been made, as Egyptian 'antiques' generally are, in a local factory, as they are in most places of the world. Alex handed it back.

"Ah, you have the trained eye," he flattered, not at all offended. "Most people do not. You take twenty for price of one. Sell to your friends. They not have trained eye."

We refused good-naturedly. "Only take what you can carry," my mother used to tell me, which meant we hardly ever bought souvenirs of any kind. The man moved on with a bow and a flourish. When I went downstairs for hats, I saw him enter the Anderssons' cabin and close the door.

We watched the loading of cotton bales for some of the time. Then we enjoyed the timeless, slow-motion dance of Port Said's canal life. It was too hot to go below except for a brief break for lunch. Finally a dusty, black, open boat was disengaged from its look-alike companions and was oared steadily across the chocolate water. Our small group boarded the dhow. All of us except for the Andersons, who, standing at the railing, the white ship as backdrop, garbed in dazzling white, held hands and seemed consumed with laughter.

The town itself offered little but heat. It was shut tight for the afternoon, as we had predicted. Shadows cast by the almost overhead sun were narrow and scarce. The streets were deserted, but everywhere else there were people sleeping: on thresholds, on open shop floors, in the little bit of shade by alley walls, in the handkerchief-sized park. It was as if someone had waved a magic wand and everyone, whatever they were doing, had stopped in mid-action to fall asleep for the afternoon.

We followed our silent guide who kept up a fast, even pace. He did not stop to talk to any of us. We kept his black robes in sight, knowing if we lost sight of him, we would never recognize him again. It seemed clear he would not recognize us, either. The children held our hands.

About five, the town began to shake off its stupor. Sleepers stretched, sat up, opened shutters and shops. Most wore traditional long black robes made of beautiful silk-like Egyptian cotton. Others wore a light-colored native style suiting, very like pajamas. At first only a few black shadows moved in the hot, white streets, mixing in slowly, like coffee in a glass of cream, then all at once the streets were thick with people.

Anxiously, I looked around for Jeff and Wyd. They were with Alex, part of another crowd gathering around the open ovens of the bread shop, one of the first places to open. A man was placing small balls of dough onto a long handled shovel with a wide, flat end. This he pushed into an oven with a roaring wood fire. In seconds the loaves had puffed up like balloons.

Our guide was out of sight. Nor could we see any of our fellow passengers.

"Let's get a bagful of loaves for the ship in case we're sent to bed without supper," I suggested, deciding to give up trying to find the guide.

The docks were now straight ahead, slightly downhill; we could see the sun shine on canal waters. We would find our own way back to the ship.

A young teenager came along on a bicycle, loudly ringing his bell. He stopped to fill an oversized tray to dizzying heights with toasty breads. First he balanced the tray precariously on his head, next he got on his bicycle, and proceeded grandly down the crowded street. Now all we could see of him over dark heads was his bobbing, tipping tray. He never bumped into anyone. He never lost a loaf.

Encouraged by this demonstration of skill, we headed back to the harbor, measuring our steps to the slow rhythm of the teeming crowds. Dozens of black-robed men offered to take us to Jessenice in their dusty dhows. Since the other passengers were not there, we selected one at random.

As we bumped against the ship, we saw a worried Stefan hovering at the top of the gangplank, two massive sailors beside him.

"Captain wants the gangplank raised." He called down, his voice showing his nervousness. "I insist we wait for you."

"That was good of you," Alex called back as we hurriedly puffed up the long gangplank.

"He say six o'clock you must be back. Other ships waiting for our berth."

As soon as we were on deck the sailors began cranking up the gangplank, but the thick hemp ropes that tied us to shore remained.

"Dinner is served at six and a half, Jeffy, Wyddy," Relief softened his furrowed face as he suggested they get ready to ring their gong.

At six-thirty we found Bjorn and Grace already seated in the hot dining room. Bjorn's face was beaded with perspiration. He laughed loudly at the report of the dull expedition.

"But I admire the Egyptians," he said, waving his fork in the air. "Sartorially speaking they are successful. They dress in pajamas all year round. When you call on them in the evening they greet you in pajamas and you have no way of knowing if they have not been in bed all day."

"Rubbish," said Harold.

"*Mais oui*! At the end of October they just lie down wherever they are and stay there for the summer. After that you have to watch your step or you will squash a sleeping Egyptian."

"Bjorn, that's good. They're like bears in reverse. They sleep all summer long," Arabella giggled.

"Why October then?" Jeff asked.

"Because that's when their summer starts," Arabella said.

"Their pajamas are beautiful," I added. "They make them with their own cotton – it's as fine as most silk. The international cotton markets grade cotton on a scale of ten. Ours is only a two on the scale. Some Egyptian cotton is ten. It glistens like silk."

"It's curious," Alex said. "The West adopted both the kimono from Japan and the pajama from Egypt, but confine their use to the bedroom. They're both styles which could have been wonderful if acceptable for other occasions."

"There was no point in getting off at Port Said," Harold said flatly. "And now there's nothing to see before we get to India."

"I wonder if the long dress the Egyptian men wear is really cooler than shorts an' short sleeves," Bertha said.

"Bombay is weeks away," Arabella said.

"Does anyone know," Alex asked, "if there is a reason why the captain would not allow us off before three?"

No one could think of anything. The children were eating cheerfully. They began to guess at riddles offered by Bjorn, laughing at the absurdity. "He who makes it, doesn't want it!" Bjorn shouted gleefully. "He who wants it doesn't need it...!"

Alex took my hand: "Feeling restless?"

"Very. Is it really true there are no more stops till Bombay?"

"That's what we were told."

"Everything's interesting if we can get to it," I said ruefully. "I wish we were stopping more often."

Stefan finished clearing the table and brought custard pudding for dessert.

"He who needs it, doesn't know it!" shouted Bjorn. "What is it? Give up. Give up! You can't guess!"

Alex and I looked at each other. I swallowed the last bite of pudding. Next time, I promised myself, we wouldn't be browbeaten by any captain's orders. Next time –

"Our son Alfie loves jokes and things like that," said Bertha. "He'd be able to figure this one out in no time."

"Stefan told me that the ship will be docked in Bombay for ten days," Alex said to me. "We'll take an inland excursion. We'll go to see the sacred caves of Ajanta and Ellora."

"After that there's Madras, Coromandel, the Malacca Straits, Singapore," I said.

"And Saigon and Hong Kong, and two ports in Japan," Alex added reassuringly. "Don't worry, the trip is bound to get more exciting."

"Give up!" Bjorn repeated loudly. "Now I tell you!"

"Okay. We give up," Jeff finally relented.

"A coffin!" Bjorn roared with laughter.

10. SUEZ CANAL

Camels for Breakfast

I awoke early next morning, aware the ship was moving. No obvious motion, just the barest forward thrust. Remembering that I had promised to wake Jeff to see our departure from Port Said, I belatedly sat up and looked out the porthole. Against the bright blur of dawn sky, eight tall, thin, furry, brown legs were walking slowly along beside us, just outside our porthole. They fell behind, but only gradually, we were going so slowly, and soon the porthole caught up with eight more.

Hurriedly. I dressed and went to the children's cabin.

"Jeff! Wyd! Wake up! Look at what's outside your porthole."

Jeff sat right up. "Wow – camels."

"Yes, camels."

Jeff couldn't take his eyes off them. "Wake up, Wyd. Wake up!"

Wyd sat up.

"Look at the camels!" He went over to the porthole to see them better. The long train of camels threaded a narrow path along the canal. Their noses lifted arrogantly in the air. "They only have to drink water once a month. They keep it in their humps."

"Where are they going?" Wyd asked, joining him on the couch to see out.

"Probably to an oasis."

"What's that?"

"It's the only place in the desert where there's water. Outside of the Nile."

"But I thought you said they didn't need water."

"I didn't say that. I just said they didn't need it very often."

"Let's go on deck," I suggested. "Maybe we'll see more of them."

"You didn't wake us up when we left Port Said," Jeff said, stripping out of his red pajamas and tugging on his shorts. "You promised."

"I overslept," I explained meekly.

"Let's go up to the Star Deck," Jeff said, in charge of the show now. "We'll see farther."

The white freighter soared high over the creamy desert. Simmering dunes smoothed out to the horizon as far as the eye could see. It was like being on a flat, round dish, which floated midway between darkness and sun.

Sailing in a convoy of a variety of other ships, as if strung out on a long line, it took two days to float across the desert. The canal itself seemed only wide enough for one ship. Wrapped in what felt like a cavity of warmth, we lay outside on deckchairs, talking about the ancient Egyptians and their ideas. One idea was that the world is flat. Here in the land where the idea had burgeoned, the concept did not seem particularly crude. It *was* flat.

We described the pyramids as we traversed the narrow ribbon of water. Although not in sight, we knew they were there, over the horizon, to starboard. Alex and I had crawled up inside them on an earlier visit and had been overwhelmed by their density, precision, incredible weight, and of course, their eternal mystery.

"Diagonally up the middle of Cheop's Pyramid," Alex remembered for the children, "the stair passage was low-ceilinged. We couldn't stand up properly. Sometimes we crawled on our hands and knees. Up and up and up, under a mass of solid stone." His red eyebrows wriggled. "You have to imagine it, kids, solid stone upon huge stone, some as big as our cabins. Imagine the weight of it. Imagine the heaviness. I couldn't breathe. I couldn't think. I was just crawling up and up."

"But," I put in eagerly, "There was a central part of the passage when we could stand up and let people coming down pass by. And further up we came to a small room, not bigger than our cabin."

"In the middle of the room was a pharaoh's sarcophagus."

"What's that?" Wyd asked.

"A king's coffin, he means," Jeff explained.

"It's carved of granite, the hardest stone." Alex went on. "And in the coffin there was a small hole, no bigger than an eye. It led out through the side of the sarcophagus, and was sited to meet up with a hole in the pyramid, itself! Some people think the pyramids were big tombs. If so, why go to the trouble of making that long, long tubular hole? Just imagine yourself lying in the sarcophagus, alone with the silence, in complete darkness. If you keep awake, and stay attentive, the moment will arrive when you witness the light of the Dog star, Sirius, shining all the way down through a hole in this massive building. You'll see it for two or three or four minutes, as it passes with infinite slowness overhead. Now, what would that weird experience do for you? If you're the Pharaoh of ancient Egypt, it will refresh and revitalize your soul. For you will feel that you have received a signal from heaven itself to go on living and guiding your great nation. A pharaoh, you see, you, and only you, have been appointed by starry Mother Night to maintain civilization in its path, and hold chaos at bay."

"By the way," I put in. "Some people think the pyramids are not just five or six thousand years old, but perhaps twenty thousand. They could have been electromagnetic arrangements made to welcome helpers from outer space. But that's another story."

Standing on the top deck, far above the sand, we caught sight of an occasional mirage of a lake in the distance. Otherwise there was nothing until we neared the wider waters of Bitter Lake situated halfway along the Canal. There we waited and watched as a long convoy of ships going north passed our own southward bound string of vessels. First came the proud passenger ships strung with colorful pennants, people waving from every deck. Next sailed freighters such as our own, laden with cargoes carefully stowed below deck. Bringing up the rear were cheery black vessels, their decks piled high with boxes and barrels, puffed up for carrying every imaginable treasure from every land of the globe. Flags of all nations, which we had begun to identify, wagged like the tails of friendly dogs. There was a great deal of shouting and honking, waving and saluting. The convoy then disappeared into the narrow northern neck of the Suez like a snake into its hole as we in turn began moving south toward the Red Sea.

The air grew thicker and hotter.

It was as if the freighter ploughed its way through melting sand. We stayed inside to enjoy what little air-conditioning there was. Then shortly before sunset, we climbed up to the Star Deck to experience the sudden evening cool.

About seven each evening the sky turned from bronze to chocolate. Our straight path of water became a ribbon of pink. A slight breeze stirred. Slowly black figures in long black robes rustled upright along the Canal's edges. The sand that had seemed smashed flat by the midday sun, now, as shadows lengthened, began to re-form into dunes. Horizontal light washed these into undulating waves of soft purples. A sliver of moon appeared in the sky. Then above, to pin it into place, one silver star. The sky seems to reach lower over deserts than anywhere else. So we could watch as one by one the sky seemed fastened with a few stars, then suddenly with thousands of stars, all the way to the horizon. Then billions. Countless. We were on a saucer with nothing but a bowlful of stars plunked upside down over us.

Later with nothing to hold the heat, the night actually got cold. But now it was still too hot to go to bed. The heat, like the legendary hand of God, pressed down hard. The four of us lay out on deckchairs, watching the play of stars and meteors, talking softly, telling each other poems and stories. We were threading our way through the same desert that Moses crossed when he led the Jews to escape their Egyptian captors. To the children it seemed quite natural to be in the place where Moses had lived, led, and legislated. To Alex and me we were living a legend.

We scanned the dark horizon as we told them how Moses had brought the Israelites up out of Egypt. When they reached the Red Sea, the waters miraculously parted. The tribe had had time to walk across dry sand to a far shore. Then mountainous waves crashed down to drown a good deal of Pharaoh's pursuing army.

"What parted the water?" Jeff asked.

"Some people say a cataclysmic volcanic eruption might have caused the seas to part," I answered. "Others say it was God who took a hand in things."

"Remember going to Santorini, kids?" Alex said. "Where we took donkeys up the side of the cliff? That is the remains of an island that now is only the shell of an ancient volcano. About the same time that Moses was escaping Egypt, Santorini erupted. It was one of the biggest natural disasters ever to take place within civilization. The gaping, smoldering hole of the Santorini caldera swallowed a billion tons of seawater, and then spewed it out again to wash huge tidal waves all around the eastern Mediterranean."

"What made Santorini erupt?" Jeff asked.

"Mum thinks the people there dug a spiral canal so that merchant ships could sail right into the island's heart, safe from winter storms. She believes sea water then seeped down, drop by drop, through the floor of the canal to the red-hot volcanic rock-layer far below. There it turned to steam and when there was enough pressure, poof! Off came the island's center like the lid off a steaming tea kettle."

Our speculations, which in those days drew laughter from many grown-ups, made perfect sense to Jeff and Wyd,

"In any case," I added. "The Jews believe that God planned it so they and Moses could escape their Egyptian captors. Even if the eruption itself was not a miracle, there's no denying the timing was.

To the minute, on time. The escaping Hebrew tribe reached safety and went over to the Sinai Peninsula without even getting wet." I gestured to the left. "Mount Sinai is just over there to port."

"If we were nearer," Alex said, "we could see it. It's one of the sacred mountains of the world. We haven't been there. But we did all get to Petra. Remember? Our guide was that Jordanian called Pharis."

As Alex reminded the children, I slipped back by myself into my own memories.

"My village is by the road, that is why they tell me to drive you," Pharis had said, as proudly as if he were leading a caravan of spice merchants across his desert. "I know the way."

To my inexperienced eye, the Jordanian desert was like crossing a well-baked matzoh. We rolled on a ribbon of grey asphalt that undulated straight from horizon to horizon under an upside-down blue bowl of sky. The desert sparkled with an ever-fresh sameness that astonished the mind.

As Pharis told it, the desert where he lived was a high plateau, gouged with deep, bone-dry riverbeds and grotesquely wind-carved ravines under which aquifers cobwebbed the cool sand, occasionally percolating up into the canyons to sustain whole villages like his own with fresh water. In the dry season, desert dwellers pitched their tents and tethered flocks in the shade of canyon cliffs, out of the way of hot winds and fierce sandstorms. In the squelching wet months, gulches and goozles might flood with dangerous suddenness. Then the high caves gave protection. At night, he said, people made fires and traded stories.

We had been driving since dawn. Now mid-morning, we were greeted by Assan, the Indian hotel owner whose unfinished hotel was the only building we had seen for hours. He stood tall on the edge of the highway, black eyes glowing like polished jet, ebony hair gnarled by desert electricity. Over brunch, Assan explained his surprising presence: "I am an astrologer. There are too many in my country to make a living."

"I'm learning astronomy," Jeff said.

"Later we'll talk," Assan smiled. Meantime, he warned, we had better go right on to our destination, Petra proper, so as to return before dark. "The entrance takes an hour to pass through. It is so narrow in the rainy season that flashing floods, you see, reach twelve feet. Seven people drowned two years ago, without rain."

"Drowned?" Alex asked.

"They were certified drowned by the police." Assan opened his palms upward. "Maybe they used buckets."

Escorted by six men in full desert robes, and led by Pharis, we mounted horses and proceeded single-file down a water-gouged gorge that zigzagged between steep red cliffs ranging up to a hundred feet in height. Only one horse at a time could squeeze through the needle narrowness. We were glad we weren't rich merchants struggling with camels.

The men kept circling us on foot.

"We see front and back – in case of water," Pharis explained, patting his pistol.

Finally, we emerged into the blazing sunshine to gaze over the vast canyon.

"Rose red Petra – half as old as time," the guard waved his arm.

We entered near the ancient Customs and Treasury, original municipal office-caves large enough to hold five hundred people. Their cavernous square rooms, cut deep into the red earth, were barren and cold. As far up and down the canyon as we could see, the cliffs were riddled with cave-dwellings whose dusty exteriors were ornamented with sculpted pediments and columns two and three stories high. The remains of hundreds of ruins, including a municipal amphitheatre, littered the canyon floor.

Once upon a time this Nabatean canyon crossroads was rich and noisy. For over a thousand years, straggling merchant caravans came from Baghdad and the north, India and the east, Egypt and the south, the Mediterranean and the west, trundling gold, glass, iron, ivory, wood, cattle, silks, and spices. They traded their customs, their stories, and sometimes their sons and daughters, too. Then trade routes shifted and Petra slipped from history. Rediscovered a millennium later, the fabled city remained inaccessible to travelers until our own day.

Few people get to the ruby city even now, yet it is never empty. Desert dwellers walk the rosy riverbed intent on their own businesses; children climb the odd-shaped rocks, playing tag, raising clouds of pink dust. Cliff-dwellers stand silently in the sunshine, silhouetted against dark cavern entrances. Their homes look comfortable, even opulent, with thick carpets and colorful cushions. At night they still make fires and trade stories.

Lilac shadows lengthened. Our escort was anxious to be off before dark. An hour later, the candlelight shining from the windows of our hotel welcomed us. We stayed out in the silver twilight for a while, stretching after the long ride. Soon there was just the disk of sandy blackness, the darker square of our hotel, and all the diamond stars visible to the naked eye spurtling down the sides of "night's inverted bowl."

Shielded from the creeping desert chill by a large paisley shawl, Assan came to stand beside Jeff and Pharis. "What is your birth sign?" he asked Jeff, continuing the earlier conversation.

"Gemini," Jeff answered. "You see those two big ones?" He pointed out two stars sparkling between troughs of darkness: "That's Gemini."

Assan followed his gaze, amazed. "I look for constellations only inside my head."

Pharis pointed to the Pleiades: "My father called those the Candelabra. He planted when the moon was in the Candelabra. But no more. He says the stars don't come back in the same months."

"He probably counted moon months." Alex said. "They have only 28 days."

"I was born in May," Pharis said. Jeff picked out his constellation, Taurus, star by star. As Pharis, and Assan too, showed interest, Jeff found Aries for them, and told stories of the Bull in the Labyrinth and the Ram's Golden Fleece.

"The constellations in your sky are like patterns on my shawl," Assan said to Jeff. He tapped his large dark forehead as he surveyed the cosmic jumble. "I will find them because I will match them now to the patterns inside my skull."

Pharis was delighted. "In my village tonight, my friends make a fire, and I tell your stories. My friends don't always like what I tell them from the city. Tonight they'll be happy. We trade good stories."

My reverie was interrupted by a sharp cough from the captain, standing stiffly beside us in full dress uniform, formal cap on, all medals in place. His two gigantic bodyguards were motionless, silent dark shadows on the moonlit deck.

We all turned to him.

"I wish to offer condolences," the captain announced without preliminaries. "From my country to yours."

Alex rose from his deck chair: "What's happened?"

"Your president has been assassinated."

His words penetrated through me slowly like a bitter and very cold drink.

"From my country to yours, I regret," the captain repeated. He shook Alex's proffered hand, bowed curtly, turned smartly and left, his two guards matching his quick step.

I was touched by his inept formality.

"Let's go below, kids. I want to find out anything else I can," Alex said.

We met Harold in the hall.

"You heard?" he asked.

"Yes. The captain just told us. Do you know how it happened?"

"Not much. Let's get Stefan to turn on the radio."

The children ran ahead to the pantry.

"I don't know what it'll mean for us," Alex said, worried. "It looks like there's already serious trouble in Malaysia, the British have washed their hands of it, and there's worse in Indonesia. Bjorn insists the U.S. is deep into Vietnam. We've taken over from the French, he says. Now how will Johnson handle it?"

"He's such a cowboy," I said. "It takes away our umbrella of security. I mean it tears the fabric of being American. I mean I don't know what I mean."

"I understand exactly. I feel it too." Alex nodded.

"But, surely the problems in the Far East will be over by the time we get there."

Jeff and Wyd came running down the corridor, ringing the gong for lunch.

"Dad," Jeff said, "the radio isn't working. Stefan says he'll get it fixed tomorrow."

We looked at each other, both tasting the sour taste that suspicion brings.

At lunch, Bjorn gleefully imparted confused and gory details of the assassination to the rest of us.

"I'm just shocked," Arabella said, white-faced. "Why should anyone want to kill that wonderful man?"

"Well, it is something one would expect might happen in the United States," Harold said.

"Why?" asked Jeff.

"It happens there all the time."

Alex broke in: "Stefan, is there more coffee?"

"Yes, Mister."

"Alex is naturally upset!" Bjorn crowed. "It's his president, after all! Now if my president were shot, I would not care. I am a citizen of the world, *oui*! I am interested in these events with the detached eye."

"You don't look upset," Grace murmured to me. "I think you are rather like Bjorn in that respect."

"When did it happen?" Harold asked. "Where was President Kennedy?"

Bjorn grinned. "Do not worry. No one will accuse *you* of the deed."

Harold tightened as if ready to spring: "Didn't you get any facts at all? Or is this just another one of your cock-and-bull stories?"

But Bjorn was addressing Jeff: "How do you feel? Are you sad? Glad? Or do you listen, like your mother and I, with the detachment of a citizen of the world?"

Jeff munched on a piece of buttered bread. "I'm not sure yet. I guess I need to know more facts first."

"Facts! Facts!" Bjorn waved his fork in the air. "So you are like Harold then. Harold likes facts. Wyd, do you like facts?"

"I love facts!" Wyd said happily.

Alex was silent, furious.

"Daddy, what's a president?" Wyd asked.

"Wyd!" Jeff was appalled. "You know what a president is!"

"I do?"

"Of course you do! The president of America is the person that everyone votes to be their leader. He's like a king," Jeff explained, the king part making concession to Wyd's greater interest in storybooks than current events. "Except that you vote for him to be your king."

"Why did they shoot him?" Wyd turned to me.

"I don't know."

"It was a madman," Bjorn said helpfully.

The term 'madman' was new to her.

"Of course you're a madman if you shoot someone!" Jeff exclaimed.

Back in the cabin for our usual afternoon reading time, we lay on one bed, snuggling closely, while I read *Alice In Wonderland* to them. I had chosen the nonsense book to fit into our lesson plan because its playful author, Lewis Carroll, had also been the famous English mathematician, Arthur Dodgson. I calmed down as I followed Alice and her curious experiences. Ideas fitted in perfectly with the morning's lesson. As Alice got bigger, or smaller, by nibbling from the caterpillar's magical mushroom, it brought back the curious nature of numbers and geometric shapes.

"She's always Alice, isn't she, big or small," I said. "Even when she's so tiny she can't reach the top of a table, or so big her head sticks out the chimney, she's still Alice."

"Of course," Jeff said, his eager voice telling me something about his sense of self, and, hopefully, his sense of security.

"There is something about Alice that remains, whatever happens to her." I went on. "Just like the shapes we were walking this morning. A square is always a square, no matter how big or small."

"Same with a circle," Jeff said to Wyd.

Their little hands outlined the shape of a square on the air above their faces.

There was something satisfying about that. Something existed even without form. Or rather, it was the invisible form that counted.

Like themselves, so to speak. The Aliceness of Alice, the squareness of a square. Also the Jeffness of Jeff, and the Wydness of Wyd.

Later I went by myself to my perch on the Star Deck, feeling a turgid flow of unease spread out the tips of fingers and toes. Alex soon found me, but even he wasn't his usual calm self.

Stefan went up to the bridge deck and headed towards Savo's radio room. On his way back, on seeing us, he climbed the stairs to where we were.

"We are all very sorry about your president. It is a terrible thing."

We nodded.

"I wished to learn more for you from Savo. He hears all reports. Your president was killed in Texas. He died immediately. They say it was one man shot him, but may be three. A man called Johnson be president. You know him?"

We shook our heads.

Together we all gazed sadly at the dancing ocean.

"Captain request your passports again. But I tell him you keep them for now?"

"Thanks, Stefan."

We watched him climb back down, grateful for his offering of concern and comfort and a small but valued token of friendship. It made us feel safer to keep our passports. Proof we *were* Americans.

For the first time we felt far from home.

11. THE RED SEA

Hostages

The Red Sea is in fact a dark oilpaint blue. We sailed out of the Suez Canal into its warm embrace. Vessels from the orient anchored near the entrance, waiting for the southbound convoys to sail through.

"I wonder why so many ships are passing ours," I said.

Even the oldest, blackest freighters in our own convoy sped past ours as soon as we were through the canal. We watched them from the shade of the passengers' deck after breakfast.

"They must be faster," Alex hazarded a guess.

"Hardly those decrepit vessels. They can't be."

But the Jessenice went slower and slower until even the motors muffled their relentless thumping. Only the softest purr was heard. The boat barely moved forward through the sweltering heat.

"When do we get to Aden?" I asked Stefan, who came to lean over the railing with us.

"We do not anchor until tomorrow afternoon." He seemed even paler than usual.

"Why are we going so slowly? At normal speed we would have been half way there by now." Alex mopped his forehead with the sleeve of his thin cotton shirt.

"The ocean gets very hot here," Stefan explained. "It be very narrow water. Too much heat collapse vacuum in motors, and cause breakdown. They explode." Heat shimmered around, hovering almost palpably on deck. "But not to worry. There is nothing to see in Aden. Not even one bug."

"How come?" I asked. A bug-less world was an admirable stretch of the imagination.

"Because there is not one drop of water for them." He shook his loose white sleeves in emphasis. "It is all in bottles."

"What a thought," Alex said. "When are they going to turn on the air-conditioning?"

"Captain makes sure the motors not get too hot," Stefan repeated.

"Tell him the air-conditioning will cool things down a bit."

"I will tell him what you say, Mister. He be good captain."

Wraithlike, he turned, receding through shimmering waves of heat.

I let my arms droop over the side of the deck rail. I wanted to touch the thick purple water far below to see how hot it was. In the sweltering mirage my arms felt long enough to reach it.

"Oceans never get so hot they feel so to the hand," Alex said, reading my mind.

"Do they make engines explode?"

We hung there, ignorant, wondering.

"Since you said you weren't going to do lessons," Alex said, "I promised the kids I'd let them teach me that game of 'Sorry'."

"I should have guessed it would be the only game aboard."

He gave me a kiss. "The kids are waiting. We'll meet you for lunch."

He went off looking for them. I had told Jeff and Wyd it was too hot for regular lessons but in fact the slow progress of the ship made me too restless to concentrate. Heading for the stairs, I paused as I saw Bjorn posing half way up the ladder to the officers' deck. He was wearing tiny pink shorts and nothing else. Black hair curled down his muscular chest and over the pink waistband. Languidly lifting one hand behind his head, elbow up, he turned smoothly, climbed the last three stairs, and danced into the corridor. Feeling a bit like Bjorn, I climbed just enough so I could see him.

He had his ear pressed against a panel of the captain's closed door.

Grace, descending in slow motion from the upper deck, smiled knowingly as she saw me move back to the rail at her approach. The sun pounded her new white dress and sandals to blinding brilliance against the clean, white freighter walls, making me squint. In her sturdy magnificence she looked like the carved prow of some ancient sailing vessel, joggled free. Or a theater prop lowered onto center stage.

I felt decidedly limp and sooty in my faded blue cotton shirt and cut-off shorts. But blue was the color I loved most, and faded like this it seemed even softer and more beautiful.

"I hope we reach Aden during the day," Grace murmured. "Shops close there at five, as they do in England."

"Have you been to Aden before?" I asked politely.

"Oh, good heavens, yes!" A slight laugh. "We've been all over the world on freighters like this." She paused looking into a personal globe of her own. "My husband is *persona non grata* in his country. He can't go home. So, well, there's absolutely nothing open in Aden until nine in the morning. British hours. We'll be gone by then. But it's very important I get off. I've arranged for special medicine for my husband to be mailed to each port."

"Medicine?"

"Yes, for my husband's tumor," Grace said with a hint of impatience, while gazing languidly into spaces unseen by me. "He was very, very sick two years ago. He was given two months to live when we met. So sad. Such a young man with so much to live for. I was his nurse. He says he got the will to live when we met. We were married immediately."

"How romantic!" I said, overenthusiastically.

"Yes, isn't it?" She replied in her usual monotone. "The medicine prevents the tumor from growing. My husband would be dead if the doctors had not discovered it."

Bjorn came up, looking excited. "Do you know no one disembarks at Aden? Captain gives orders. Stefan is responsible for making sure none of us escape. Captain says he will be shot if we escape. A most unhappy fate for our poor steward."

Grace did not seem to hear. Still in slow motion, she left. I turned back to the sea, hoping Bjorn would go too. Images of Africa, just over the horizon, invaded my consciousness, undulating in and out with the indecisiveness of the schools of spineless jellyfish gathering about our ship's hull.

Bjorn went on talking. He must have come to terms with death a long time ago, I thought. He has a time bomb in his brain, the fuse lit and about to explode. Does he think about it? Is that why everything is a game to him?

"You know what my friend the third mate tells me?" Bjorn moved closer. The thick smell of suntan oil and perspiration oozed from his smoothly tanned skin. I leaned over the sun-warmed rail. He was a spiritual octopus with tentacles of fear, and the air around him became dark with unease.

"Arabella kill her husband because he sleeps with another man. Did you know he was her psychiatrist? He gave her pills to make her more svelte. They drove her crazy. They are no longer allowed on the marketplace. They must be very bad to make her kill him. They had been married fifteen years." He sighed. "Can you imagine, Jane, fifteen years with Arabella?"

"No."

"Captain tells my friend third mate not to have intercourse with me. My friend refuses, of course. He has powerful friends in his country. Captain scream at him. Really, Jane, our captain is a very offensive man. Yesterday he stood outside my cabin with the second mate for half an hour. They listened at my door! I know, because I watched all the time from the end of the corridor."

I propped my chin on my arms. The sea was calm. Did Grace marry him because he was going to die? When the drugs wear off because he cannot get them, does he think about it? Does the game get put away like a game of 'Sorry,' sometimes?

* * *

Late afternoon the next day, our little family was again on the topmost deck to watch our arrival at Aden Harbor. Harold and Bertha joined us.

"The steward says there's no reason for us to get off," said Harold, "but I'm a bit curious just the same."

"If nothing else," added Bertha, "I'm ready for a break. It'd be nice to see flowers."

"It'd be nice to talk to some British blokes," Harold said.

"Don't you think people must 'ave gardens in Aden?" said Bertha. "Someone's got to have a garden. It's British, you know."

"Or maybe even a park?" Harold said.

"I don't know," I said, "but I'm longing to see a place with no bugs."

"Our son Alfie doesn't like bugs either. Remember how 'e 'ates earwigs, 'Arry?"

"Why are we stopping here, if no one's allowed off?" Jeff asked.

"We'll stop to bunker," Alex explained.

"What's that?" Wyd asked.

"Refueling. This is the refueling stop for ships going to or from the Orient. They pipe diesel fuel out from shore to the bunkers where the ships tie up."

Bit by bit, we began to make out the bunkering island with its white buildings, causeways, and docks.

An enormous ship was docked fairly close to shore.

"I thought the place was supposed to be big," I said.

Alex shaded his eyes, puzzled.

"It's not really that small."

"But that one ship takes up almost everything."

"It must be an optical illusion."

But as the Jessenice nosed nearer, the ship grew larger – larger, until it seemed monstrous in proportion to our own.

"It's American, isn't it?" Jeff said. "I can see the flag."

"It certainly is American," Harold sniffed. "Ridiculous!"

The majestic freighter we were on had shrunk to proportions so small that we fitted right under the jutting flight deck of the great monster ark.

We read the huge letters on its stern: *U.S.S. Essex* – one of our titanic aircraft carriers. All the carrier's portholes were locked against the heat, far too high up to see into in any event. They were tiny from so far away. The underside of the deck was pinned together by giant bolts as big as cars. Jeff liked that.

In spite of the intense heat, I shivered.

"It's your *Essex*, isn't it?" Harold said. "Why are we bunkering so close?"

"Maybe to pretend we have nothing to fear but fear itself," Alex said.

Tension aboard ship heightened as the freighter settled almost to a stop. The officers were visibly unnerved. They walked white-faced and quickly, heads averted. The hot evening sky flared ominously red around the edges of the flight deck overhead.

Bjorn bounced over to join us, trailing a nervous Arabella.

"Not even crew is allowed off," he told us cheerfully. "Captain's orders."

"Stuff the orders," Alex growled.

Arabella pursed her scarlet lips. "Honey, the captain's word is law on a ship. Even you should know that."

In spite of the captain's order, water-taxies hovered hopefully nearby. We were not more than fifty yards from our berth.

Alex met my eyes and made a gesture I understood.

"Kids," I said, "let's go get ready for lunch."

They ran ahead. By ourselves in our cabin Alex spoke with some urgency: "I bet we're carrying explosives. And if they were to blow, then the underwater fuel pipes would go as well, and probably the Essex! It'll make the Santorini Island explosion seem like a pop gun."

"But the port authorities wouldn't allow us to bunker with explosives."

"Not if they knew."

I felt a little faint. "Explains it all. So we're not allowed off so we won't talk to anyone."

"It also means we've got to deliver the damn things to some country down the road. I'm going to check our papers right now."

Our locked briefcase lay where we had left it in the bottom drawer of our closet. Its lock was broken and our passports were missing. We went through every envelope, every paper; then hunted the room.

Alex was livid.

"Let's find the captain."

We went to the steps leading to the bridge. Sweating, Mikhail, the giant bosun, blocked our way.

"I want to see Captain Stanislav," Alex said.

They eyed each other belligerently.

Mikhail took a step backwards, shaking his large head. "He be very busy."

Then, turning swiftly for so huge a man, he climbed up to the bridge.

"At least he noticed us," Alex said unexpectedly. "I'll make a friend of him yet."

"I'll talk to Stefan," I said.

"Good idea. Go ahead."

Stefan was seated on his stool in the corner of his pantry, almost as though he was waiting for me.

"Please, Missus. Do not disturb captain now."

"He took our passports."

"On board ship Captain keep all passports."

"Then he has to give us day passes. We're being kept prisoner."

"It be too dangerous."

"More dangerous than on board? Aren't you afraid for the children?"

"I am afraid for you, too," he answered, softly. "But, Missus, you cannot get off the ship. Tomorrow you have passports. I promise this."

"Tomorrow I won't need them."

"Missus, he be good captain. He not make mistakes." Stefan took a deep breath: "It be dangerous here. You see those pipes under water? He make one inch mistake, one inch and they crack. Catastrophe. Please do not disturb him. We be in Bombay soon."

"Those pipes are why I want my kids off."

"I understand. But he not make mistakes. This no time to talk to captain. Please." His dark eyes held mine: "Please Missus, if you be in real danger, I help. But if I bother captain now, I may not help you later."

I stepped back, confused.

"Okay, Stefan. But I'm doing this for you. Not for the captain."

Stefan nodded his head and slowly seemed to relax. He shook his neck to loosen the tension, then his shoulders, slowly rotated his arms and wrists. His knees swung a little; his ankles revolved in place. His toes probably twirled too. He had relaxed.

Sometime about midnight, I stood alone on my Star Deck, midway between the radioactive threat overhead and the explosive harbor below. Absorbed by the very boringness of the danger, I slipped into a trance-like acceptance of my perilous position, watching the Jessenice back up and begin to slowly make a circle over the maze of thick pipes – fat underwater tubes flowing with oil which shone like tentacles from monster sea creatures just inches from our hull. Silver fish glistened in and out of their grasp. There was no margin for error. Out of sight of the Americans overhead as it circled directly beneath the Essex's enormous flight deck, the Jessenice hardly seemed to move at all. Glacier slow, she did not edge beyond an invisible circle the captain had drawn for himself. Flood lamps on the Essex shone overhead, too high to shed light on the green water where Jessenice was so noiselessly rotating.

Harbor lights dimmed, docks fell silent. Boats drifted off. One of our searchlights glanced off our prow, beaming onto our gangplank, then throwing a perfect circle of light onto the emerald water.

What was I doing there in the middle of the night, under threat of possible extinction, on the other side of the world?

Silence thickened the air. Monotonous as it was, with only the tiniest of movements to witness, still I could not leave my bird-like perch. Beneath the boat monstrous creatures swam, some alive, some technical. I was hypnotized by the mysteries of the unknown; also the mysteries of the unknowable.

Some two hours later, the glacial circling stopped and we inched out from under the Essex into our own bunkering slot. Now I could see the night sky straight above me. Two white-faced crewmen surfaced from below deck. Anchors roared over the side. Without a word to me, the sailors passed on their way back to their quarters.

Motors stilled. The port stilled, Essex was still, and now the Jessenice drifted to stillness.

Still I did not leave. The sky was so clear it was easy to distinguish all the colors of the stars. Tonight they did not sparkle like clear tears and spears of song, but in colors, like a king's dream of tourmalines.

Alone, attached to the stars, it all seemed fated, determined, intensely reasoned. The one line of one person's life had circled into this moment, and all life had circled there; all of the long evolution of earth, the patient rounds of planets and stars, the ever larger arcs of clusters and galaxies had spiraled down, a snail-shell of stars and time, to this point, this moment.

I no longer wondered what I was doing there. I expanded, about to burst or shout with the happiness of being under all those blue and purple and green and yellow suns at the other end of the world.

12. ARABIAN SEA

Under the Continent with No Name

The ship left Aden at night, while the passengers slept. The next morning I took the children out on deck for a lesson in arithmetic. I had chosen arithmetic because its formal beauty would serve to counter any puzzlement and anger I felt at the captain.

"Here, each of you take a piece of chalk. Pick which color you like."

Red for Jeff.

Yellow for Wyd.

Green for me.

"Now follow the marks I make. First you, Jeff."

I drew a square on the deck boards. Jeff followed the light mark with a hefty red one. Next I outlined a triangle: Wyd went over it. With a final flourish a sea-green pentagon appeared, its sides about the same length as the other two figures. The pattern looked like some magical symbol shining in the sunshine. I was as riveted as the children.

"Now, let's count to a hundred, but in a new way. Wyd, say one number to yourself and one number out loud. All the way up. Jeff, you say two numbers to yourself and then one out loud. I'm going to say four to myself and one out loud. Let's see what happens."

"I know – they'll meet," Jeff said immediately.

I lifted my brows wonderingly. "Let's see. Let's also see if we can walk around these lines without bumping, while we're counting. You take the triangle, Wyd. I'll take the five sides. A pentagon we call it, like *pente*, in your Greek. You take the red one, Jeff."

"The red square." He jumped into place.

"Okay. Say the numbers, walk slowly, and don't bump."

The spaces entered through their bones, rather than through their heads. Later geometry would not appear to them as a fortress to storm, but as a habitable house. The children laughed with surprise each time their voices blended out loud. They moved as in some mysterious dance, some arcane rite, slowly counting the paces. Then we counted all the way back from a hundred, still by twos, threes, and fours.

Numbers are usually so thin and squeezed, I thought, deeply involved in the process. You feel tippy looking at them, as if you might fall off. They do not seem strong enough to stand on. And when you get a line of them all together, they seem scrunched and leaning to one side. Your shoulders get hunched just thinking about them.

I wanted the children to know something extraordinary about numbers. I wanted them to hold the numbers, give them room to stand and breathe, and then know how each felt. For instance, I thought, reaching the beginning again, 'one' is not a lonely, naked, chilly thing on a page. 'One' is a whole pumpkin at Halloween, or a stocking at Christmas. Maybe an Earth. And, first of all, the universe.

Do something big when you want to move on from one. Maybe separate light from darkness.

Sometimes as we counted backwards we traced the patterns backwards also. We could do it without bumping, even with our eyes closed, because we could trust the patterns to hold us in place. The children were light on their feet, pulled together in happy concentration.

When it got too hot to stay on deck, they went downstairs to write in their books. Wanting to be alone for a while, I found a patch of shade behind a funnel where I hoped no one would find me. I felt clear-sighted, floating above the ship, gazing at the images of the desert as if everything were still there, which it was – not so long ago either – only some ten, twelve thousand years or so. The great glaciers of the last hundred thousand years-long Ice Age had pretty much melted. A major cataclysm had followed. Rising water created entirely new seas, notably the Irish Sea and the Bering Sea; and thundered through the Pillars of Hercules at the entrance to the Mediterranean to inundate its coasts, to sink whole cities and villages. It was a memorable flood. Some people still look for Noah's ark atop Mount Ararat in Turkey. That's pretty high up. Now we were sailing out of the Gulf of Aden, around Sinai, into the Arabian Sea. A good deal of the Arabian continent we were bounding under had once been partly submerged. Other parts became fertile beyond measure. One part was called the Garden of Paradise, and the Four Rivers of Paradise were said to run through it. The Hanging Gardens of Babylon flourished. The Tower of Babel rose there.

Why do I say "not so long ago, only some ten, twelve thousand years?" Imagine it – it's an amount of time. After almost a month aboard ship, I was beginning to wonder whether I could weather even our little journey of seven months. Trying to imagine ten thousand years was … Well, try it. From my solitary, funnel-forested perch, I gave up trying and instead watched instead only the sky and water.

Wind and waves had shed almost all signs of bronze sky, golden sand, and ochre dust. Blue, now. All was blue, which is more a transparency than a color. Sky was faraway da Vinci blue; water had returned to a Vermeer blue, without any black or white in it at all. Then waves began forming into fairly large pyramids of midnight purple-blue that we could slide up and down to our great delight. No white froth.

Now if we looked at the globe in our cabin, we could think of ourselves as galloping below Iran which Alex and I had visited a couple of years before. Iran, Afghanistan, and Pakistan are central to the Continent with No Name. Iraq, too, since it incorporates ancient Sumer, the earliest and most seminal of ancient civilizations.

Iran used to be called Persia, and its empire of elegance and cultivation sparkled far and wide across the continent. But like a glass of spilt milk, empires have a way of ending their expansion. The 'freedom loving' Greeks are still famous for upsetting the ancient Persian cup of milk at Marathon, stopping Xerxes from any more conquest, and making a statement for freedom that has lasted some two and a half thousand years.

My attention was on water, but my imagination pulled me down dark eons, just as the White Rabbit did with Alice down the well. I could see how it was that when Europe had wrung out its mile-high glacier blankets, it also fogged the world's atmosphere so that faraway plains sprang up fresh and fertile, and for millennia forests grew which now are deserts. Peoples began to migrate from as far away as Europe and Mongolia, first to graze their animals, then to farm, finally to settle.

I slipped from imagining to remembering . . .

We were driving across the undulating plain of Persepolis in southern Iran. We had been visiting what remains of Xerxes' palace, a high stone terrace with a few columns rising some thirty feet into the hot air, plus carved bas-reliefs of lions attacking bulls which flanked the winding grand staircase, and rather a lot of huge friezes of Xerxes being honored with long lines of conquered peoples bringing presents. Xerxes used to set up his winter quarters here, consisting mostly of gorgeous Persian silk tents, cushions, and carpets.

Xerxes' empire stretched "from India even unto Ethiopia," as the Bible says. Then he was eager to take on the 'freedom loving' Greeks. To everyone's delight, and as everyone knows, he lost ignominiously.

The narrow asphalt road scrolled up behind us, but still arrowed straight north to south as far as the eyes could see. A soft fuzz of dry grass covered the barren earth on both sides. What seemed to be a ridge in the road ahead started to undulate across our asphalt ribbon, stretching west to east as far horizons. As we came closer, we discerned caravans, camels, and men, pregnant women, then children, goats, chickens. They carried all they possessed.

We stopped, unable to pass for almost an hour. Kurdish nomads were migrating south to winter grazing lands, as had their ancestors from time immemorial. They walked firmly, six or seven abreast, in extended family clusters, each caring for its own. All were burdened according to their capacities. During the two hours we waited, I saw only one small child stop to pee. But two women in labor, and a full-term donkey were taken behind some nearby rocks without ado. When they reappeared about twenty minutes later with their newborns, mother and offspring were each tenderly tied atop a mule to catch up with their family group. Finally, a kindly patriarch, regal atop a tiny grey donkey, arranged a break in the line. Impassively, we were bowed through.

We sped on to Pasagardae, where Cyrus, King of Kings, is buried. It was late afternoon when we arrived onto the desolate, grey plain from where Cyrus, one of the most powerful conquerors of all time, once ruled the Continent with No Name.

Alex and I usually don't go to tombs of conquerors because once you've seen one, you get déjà vu "all over again" at the next one. But this time, for a couple of hours, we wandered Pasagardae. Dry ravines were scored deeply into barren grey-green mountains that encircled a large plain like a giant moldy doughnut, sinister against a grey-green sky. No one else was there. Nothing was left of Cyrus the Great but his simple sepulcher, no larger than the ship's lounge. It had been robbed by the troops of Alexander the Great over 2000 years before we got there. When Alexander heard that his troops had ransacked it, he had them punished harshly, and the tomb restored. But that was after he had conquered the Persian Empire, and was himself ruling 'from India even unto Ethiopia.'

Cyrus' last request was carved in stone:

I am Cyrus, King of Kings. Do not begrudge me these few feet of earth.

Other graves crowded around Cyrus. But not many. To this day, migrating nomads circle his sepulcher each year as they travel back to winter quarters. They leave bowls of mare's milk on the steps before moving on.

In the center of the darkening plain, brooding over the awesome emptiness, two white storks nested atop an antenna soaring some fifty feet into the grey-green twilight. We floated on a segment of time broken off a chunk of thousands of years.

Back aboard ship, floating on my smooth sailing memory device, Star Deck, I watched the Nomads marry, have children, work hard, seed much of our western culture, and worship their own gods and goddesses. Feeling safe enough, some began large-scale trading, sending caravans north and south, east and west. I watched as poets, seekers, seers joined these mobile merchants, mixing their stories, poems, and art, not only across nations, but across tribes, religions, ages, and classes. The most remarkable of these freshening lifelines was the Silk Road, a caravan route that connected China to the Mediterranean, with offshoots north and south, one of which led through ancient Petra to Egypt, and half way down the Red Sea coast of Africa to create the Blue Bead Route to Britain.

As time passed, over thousands of years, the sun shone ever hotter on this heartland, which began to dry up. There was urgent incentive to bring water to parching fields and thirsty villages. Mountain streams were made to run through labyrinthine brick channels and mountain caves and tunnels which served to irrigate and fertilize vast plains below. It made me think of two of the labors of Herakles: the first, his inventive way of cleaning King Augeaus' stables by damming a mountain stream so that it branched out to run through Augeaus' extensive stables and wash them clean. The second was his fight with Achelous, the Greek River God. He used the same method on the Achelous River as he had on the King's stables: by breaking a horn off the River God, he created an irrigation canal, from which smaller channels were made to branch off so that a cornucopia of fruits and vegetables would bloom in the dry fields. In effect, the myth of Herakles was a newspaper story bringing news of the discovery of hydraulic-engineering and irrigation to Ancient Greece.

As climates changed, sophisticated irrigation kept things growing. The ziggurat Tower of Babel – The Tower of Many Tongues – continued its rise toward Ahura Mazdao, the God of Light, whose shadow was now manifesting the nature of time.

Three modern-day world religions spun out from this land: first Judaism, with Christianity and Islam following each in turn. All preached "the One God." Or one Good. Or one good after another. And yet they have divided rather than united as they killed one another.

Conquerors insist on only One God, describing that Being as Top Dog. Through conquest they carry their own rules and religions with them, ponderously imposing them on the conquered as they pursue their bloody ways. Conquest is always brutal, always despoiling sandcastles not built in a day. Those fleeing the iron chariots go lightly, carrying their songs, chants, and stories with them. Usually their culture and religion is often all they carry – that and their children.

Tyrants coerce, whereas poets, artists, storytellers sing the daily life, the immediate life, the only life we have, the one we love. Jelaluddin Rumi, one of the supremely great poet-sons of the Continent with No Name, is an example of such creative mixing. Born at Balkh, (now in Afghanistan) he was exiled by the Mongols, and walked to the other end of the Silk Road to settle in Konya, Turkey. Rumi spoke in Turkic, wrote in Persian, and chanted the holy Qu'ran as it was written, in Arabic.

A vivid memory catches your soul as a dream-catcher catches your dreams. This is particularly so sailing across wide expanses of oceans. It's all dream, immediate experience, and memory. If you're not interrupted, you can sort things out and drop a lot overboard.

Idly from my vantage point, I watched Bjorn round a corner, tiptoeing in and out of the deck shadows. He had been spending the last few days sunning himself and his tan had deepened to a rich cherry-wood stain. He was looking for someone. I hoped it wasn't me.

Like an animal in the jungle, he felt my eyes and looked up. A few minutes later, he climbed the ladder and waved cheerfully.

"Ah, there you are! I have been searching all over for you. I looked into your cabin. Only Alex is reading there."

"Hello, Bjorn."

"It is crazy voyage we all are taking, is it not? It is best for us all to be friends. Harold does not understand this, but he is uneducated. You and I, we understand each other. You are intelligent. The officers," he went on without taking a breath, "know everything about the passengers. Before we are allowed on board we are all very thoroughly checked."

"I'm not sure they did a thorough job this time."

"Jane, do not be naïve. I am sure Harold has told you about their son, Alfie. He died a year ago, very unexpectedly. They refuse to talk to me about it. Bertha did not take it well. She takes to the bottle instead."

"That sounds very sad."

"Yes, but Jane... And poor Harold, too, *non*?" Bjorn tapped the side of his head. "The war. This is why Bertha is always how you say 'squift?' It is a most amusing theater, I think."

"You should have been a private investigator. Nothing gets by you"

He gave a wink. "Better than *un petit investigateur*. I am in manu-are."

"It's too hot up here. I'm going below."

"I like Alex. Yes, I do. But your soul is deep and mysterious. I see this at once. It is for the children you stay with him. I understand this, *oui*. I have children. Their mother will not let me see them."

I edged away and, following me, Bjorn changed tack. "Do you know how sick I was? I was dying. Everyone said I would die. I fooled them. Yes, one day I said to myself I will live, and I will fool them all. I walked out of the hospital. I will not consult a doctor again. *Non*, they are quacks. But this is true with cancer: you need the will to live and – *voila!* The cancer vanishes. I am living."

He flexed a bicep, glancing fondly, his interest diverted, he went downstairs.

93

I decided to remain where I was. Before long, I was sucked once again into the three-dimensional deeps of memory…

After a week in the museums and bazaars of Teheran, and seven hours bumping over barely roads in an open Jeep across the hot, colorful deserts of western Iran, we found ourselves stumbling up a mountain in the footsteps of our host: Iran's head archaeologist, Ezat Neghaban. We were on a fast three-hour mid-afternoon climb around and over silver rice paddies in golden fields, leading to Neghaban's still secret excavation site called Marlik. Panting and sweating, we finally halted atop a dome-shaped tumulus, a burial mound some hundred feet wide and nearly three thousand years old. The pungent fragrance of Iranian anise filled the air.

Marlik had once been a gateway city to and from the West by way of the southern edge of the Caspian Sea. Taxes and duties, inns, and store-houses had made the strategic city and its royal family rich.

We were asked to stand in the sun until we stopped panting and sweating, then Ezat's two assistants welcomed us into the shade with a mound of white rice made savory with an abundance of fresh anise and local butter, plus a glass of water served at midday-temperature. A dozen armed guards stood casually around a low, windowless, rectangular cement-block building, backs politely turned to us, rifles at the ready. For this tiny fortress was a modern day Aladdin's Cave. As Ezat showed us into the gloom of one dim electric light, he pointed out that floors and shelves of its three rooms were littered with fragile, pre-Homeric ceramics. A commercial-size fridge stood right beside the door, wrapped with heavy steel chain. Lengths of red ribbon had been added, and the whole stamped with an imposing wax seal culled from the dig. Without so much as an 'Open Sesame,' Ezat broke the seal, unwrapped the yards of red ribbon, and unlocked the steel chain. He slowed down as he opened the door to our bedazzled eyes: pre-Homeric jewelry, embossed golden goblets, cups, bowls, and some of the world's first ornamental cavalry accoutrements shone out into the room. All were of the finest workmanship. Then as we thrilled to the timeless display, Neghaban offered each piece for hands-on scrutiny.

When night fell, Aladdin's treasure was returned to its fridge. Alex and I went outside to seek the hole in the ground that served for toilet. Even with the lights off, we could see in the dark, because the outside world is never totally dark. There's moonlight, or there's starlight, or stardust at least, as on this night.

Ezat's two assistants retired to the back room, closing their door by the time we returned. Offering each of us a candle, our host showed us to our sleeping quarters in the windowless room between theirs and his in front. A narrow path snaked to our cots through a mass of precious artifacts – male and female ceramic and glass figures mostly, about two feet high, and very breakable. Courteously, Ezat took our candles, warning us of grave-serpents as he left us in darkness. He would sleep with his fridge. He kept the door between us unlocked. But he loudly bolted the way to the outside.

We were left in dark silence. There was not a sound to direct our imaginations. Darker than a closet with the door closed. Darker than your eyes closed. One color of black. Not even a color. More like a porous-ness – a darkness that could be felt. Palpable obscurity.

"Alex, put your hand in front of your eyes," I whispered.

"I can't even see it!" he said.

"Me, too! It's darkness right up to the eyeballs. There's no space in front. It's like there's no body."

Hardly daring to move, yet not daring not to, I whispered: "I'm putting my hand out. Not down, straight out. Okay?"

Reaching straight out and moving back and forth a bit, but not down, we found each other's hands. We felt our currents coursing between us in the dark middle.

I was not able to offer prayer to even one of the three "One Gods" that night.

13. EAST OF ADEN

Living History

The heat intensified. The Arabian Sea was rough, and some of the passengers stayed queasily in their cabins. I no longer conducted any lessons indoors; the children carried on with their schoolwork in the hot shade of the cabin deck. It was fresher outside than in the cabins since the captain still did not turn on the air-conditioning.

"Do you know that these crystals are all cubes, like little elf-blocks?" I said.

The sailors had hosed the decks down with salt water. The sun had dried them so now they were covered with salt crystals. The children knelt on deck to examine them.

"Can I get the magnifying glass?" Jeff asked. "I can't see anything this way."

"Good idea."

He bounded away. When he returned we stretched out on our stomachs to watch the magical crystalline sparkles on the deck. The morning lesson passed mostly in silence. Once the captain had to step over us, grunting disapproval.

Alex joined us eventually and we sat up to dangle our feet over the side of the boat, watching the dazzling rainbow sparkle of flying fish. The smack of the prow thumping along at full speed drove clusters of the winged creatures out of the water. Each group flew for a minute or more, their silver traces marking the air to the back of the ship, there to mingle with the circling of the seagulls and the lacy curls of the wake.

We were sailing East of Aden to Bombay and it would take about seven days. The vast landmass to the north of us was not all a mystery to us. Alex and I had visited a good deal of it on magazine assignments at one time or another.

The whole thing was more a living picture of geography and history. It harbored more than a dozen distinctive peoples. Yet they shared the one identity of time and place: like each other, say, with characteristic differences, rather like those between a Vermonter and a Texan – both American. But this Mid-Asian Continent with No Name, as I called it, resembles America in size. Except that it has nations instead of states, and does not enjoy the protection of one well-guarded boundary. Nor does it have one federal government dispensing fairly equal justice; nor one set of federal laws; nor one currency, nor just one military. Instead, there's nationalism, racism, repression, and burning embers of revolution.

Over thousands of years, traders, conquerors, pilgrims, teachers, have crisscrossed this continent, moving along dangerous ways and byways to storied cities worth every hard, hot step. From Kabul to Istanbul; from Karachi to Damascus, Marlik to Mecca; from Babylon to Balkh and Baghdad, from Persepolis to Petra.

All jewels in the crown of the Continent with No Name.

"Imagine these traders and their caravans," Alex told the kids. "Traversing their vast purple-amber sands, like sailors sailing the oceans. It's best to travel by the cool of night. They were guided by the fixed stars, as well as by the moon and the planets, and by the sun in the daytime. Those features move around, some swiftly and some slowly, so travelers had to learn, and record, and remember, their sky patterns of movement. How did they do it? By telling each other myths and legends which touched, again and again, upon deep space, star-time measurements, and numbers."

"No wonder they were good at arithmetic," Jeff said.

"Imagine," Alex went on, "Those hardy traders settling comfortably in the open courtyards of welcoming inns, inhaling the fragrant smoke of succulent dinners simmering over open fires, tasting fragrant wines. I see them intermingling with the eagerness of strangers. They tune their ears to the soft plash of fountain waters – and new languages. There are always triumphs and tragedies to share: a word to the wise, an orange cart to upset, a treasure to be found, a king to avoid, a bandit to befriend. The intercourse between these wide-wanderers tended to be original, metaphysical, and eminently practical. Characteristically, all three at once. Softly, the people of the book, and the people of the stars, lonely, tired travelers in faraway places, swapped their twice-told tales. The ones with wisdom, the ones with humor, the ones cynical, the ones sacred, the ones evolutionary, the ones revolutionary."

Wyd in particular was entranced by his images.

We were now sailing east of Eden. Well, Aden – because Eden lies hidden from the secular mindset of today, which prefers to forget that some of our earliest legends actually took place in real time. Language has a way of remembering, and safely conveying treasures from times long gone. So we were sailing east of Eden, happily following currents of timeless time and spaceless space, towards a place to which we all belong, contribute to, and breathe in and out continually – breathing something different than air, "it" being consciousness, not oxygen.

To be sure that we knew where we were in the floating world, I showed the kids my favorite Chinese hieroglyph for 'seeing' – an eye on legs. "Put your eyes on legs, and let's walk around the Continent with No Name."

"Okay," Alex said. "We'll start at Sinai's peninsula. Then we'll follow the road up through the Golden Crescent lands of the eastern Mediterranean, all the way to Istanbul. The Greeks call it Constantinople, after the first Christian Roman Emperor, Constantine who moved his court there from Rome."

"But Alex, now the Turks call it Istanbul. Istanbul is actually a question: 'To the city?' Apparently migrating Greeks were forever asking the way 'stin polis?' 'to the city?' It's colloquial."

"Be that as it may," Alex said with obvious disbelief, "the city is strategically positioned on both the east and west banks of the entrance to the narrow Bosphorus. Thus it stands in both Europe and Asia, astride their spiritual dividing line."

"I'll get the globe," Jeff said firmly.

As we waited for him to get back, watching the blue water, I remembered silently the great Church of Constantine:

I had stopped against the last three rungs at the top of the ancient iron fire ladder, almost half way between the floor and the top of the dome in the Mother of all Churches: Aghia Sophia. I was alone. Well, not exactly alone. If I looked straight down five stories, I could see Alex leaning against an enormous iron wheel seemingly to keep it from moving. Beside him Abdul, glowing in a white linen suit topped with a wide-brimmed white Panama hat, locked it in place. Another six men, in dark grey work-clothes, receded anonymously into thicker shadows around the fire ladder's base.

Under these conditions, it's better to look up. Above me floated the most influential dome in architecture, its crown lost in darkness some five stories beyond my ladder's end. A ring of forty thick stone ribs separated by arched glass windows defined the circumference of the dome's immense base. If I could have stretched my arms fifty feet to either side of my lofty perch, I could have touched the base of the great arched walls. There was nothing in the way. I was floating in space scooped out from infinity by the architects Anthemios and Isidorus, then held in place for some fourteen centuries essentially by the integrity of their mighty design. Many thousands can fit into

Aghia Sophia at one time and they have, whether to worship or to seek sanctuary in time of wars, witch-hunts, crusades, conquests, riots and restorations – separately and together.

From the grandeur of Istanbul's Blue Mosque down to the tiniest of Christian churches sprinkled like sugar cubes across the thyme-purpled landscape of the eastern Mediterranean, to the Duomo of Florence, Saint Paul's Cathedral in London, and our own Capitol in Washington, all were birthed by glorious Aghia Sophia.

Little remains of its fabled Byzantine embellishments. Gone are the emperors in their golden robes, followed by their trains of sugar-stuffed courtiers playing with their golden mechanical toys. Gone, too, are the great silver iconostasis and the golden altar. A few of the frescoes and mosaics remain. History's dark shadows are still wrapped around porphyry columns once stolen from pagan temples. Shadows penetrate the gouged eyes of frescoed saints; they encircled the great green discs from which the golden name of Allah glows; they blur the edges of holy space now become secular. Yet nothing important is missing.

"Do you wish to go higher?" Abdul's voice floated up.

"This is fine." My voice floated down.

I had met Abdul two hours earlier when I looked into the two pools of dark amber that were his eyes as he said firmly: "Aghia Sophia is closed for ten days' repairs." We had taken the morning flight up from Greece. Alex was writing an article on Istanbul. But there was to be no entrance into the great church. No way. That was Abdul's position.

"You are Americans, You live in Hollywood. All Americans live in Hollywood," he changed the subject after half an hour of us trying to persuade him to let us in. "You make my photograph. Carry it to Hollywood. My dream is to be a movie star."

"Closed?" My mind was on the church.

"Closed." He shook his white sleeves to show they were empty. His mind was on Hollywood.

You cannot tell about other people's dreams, nor anticipate the accidents of life.

I agreed to photograph him. I had only one roll of twelve Roliflex negatives with me, but obviously closed meant closed. I'd get more later. Abdul posed happily against the front doors: Voluptuous lips wet: Victor Mature. Click. Eyes squinting with passion: Rudolf Valentino. Click. Profile, nose in air: John Barrymore. Click. Deadpan, George Raft. Click. Eyelids veiling the goodness of his heart in an evil world: Humphrey Bogart. Click. About to open the door: Charles Boyer. Click. One hand in pocket, murderous: Edward G Robinson. Click. Vacuous: Robert Taylor. Click. Eyebrows meeting in a steeple: Don Ameche. Click. About to bring the chili rellenos: Cesar Romero. Closeup: Hat at a rakish angle, one shoulder forward, intense: Abdul himself. Click. Eleven pictures done

I kept back one for good luck.

"Wait here," Abdul ordered. A fidgety twenty minutes later, the fire ladder platform was rolled up to the three story sized bronze doors by six panting 'Istanbullions'. The base held a folded iron ladder pointing up into the air about eight feet. It was wrapped in cloth rags. "The iron gets too hot for the hands in a fire." Abdul explained. The ungainly machine ran silently on two eight-foot high, rubber-sheathed wheels

"Our machinery is not up to date, but we take good care of it," Abdul said proudly.

Pulling out an iron key about a foot long, Abdul slid it into the great front door keyhole, turning it with both hands. The doors slid open on well-oiled hinges. "Go in," he motioned. There was no electric light – only grey shadows on silver atoms. We had the entire church to ourselves. The men rolled their machine into the center under the dome, and cranked the ladder straight up. When it reached some five stories up into the luminous dark, they stopped and turned to me.

"You can go take pictures." Abdul smiled the gratitude that knows no bounds.

I climbed the shaky rungs to where the ladder ended in mid-air, my Roliflex with its one negative dangling from my neck. I floated in space scooped out from infinity and, hanging on with one hand I lifted my camera. The click rolled down the dome, the semi-domes, and the quarter-domes. I wound and clicked the now empty camera a dozen times more so Abdul would hear and not call me down. I became the still camera and the thirteenth negative. Shadows, space and silence were silver-printed on my soul.

Meanwhile, Jeff returned with his globe.

I wanted to get the whole "Continent with No Name" into one image so Jeff and Wyd could get a whole idea of it; as we have of North America with all its states. Istanbul only pins down my Continent with No Name on its northwest corner. On its strategic eastern banks, I said to the children, imagine buying a couple of little Greek donkeys. You can ride them when you get tired.

"Greeks say that when you get to heaven," Wyd interrupted, "you'll find it filled with their donkeys, because they are so patient and good."

"That sounds true and beautiful," I agreed.

"Let's sit in the shade so we can all see your globe, Jeff," Alex said. "We'll begin where we left off, at Istanbul. Proceed east through Turkey. Later you can change to horses, and keep your donkeys to carry things. Go east to upper Kurdish pasturelands, stitching up and down the petticoat fringes of Russia: Armenia, Georgia. Make a dip south and you'll be crossing ancient Sumer. That was in Iran. It's a good spot to stop at a crossroads market on the Silk Road, to buy a camel or two at auction. We'll keep the donkey and the horses, and ride camels across Iran and go on as far east as Afghanistan. From there we'll go to the great markets at Balkh, and pick up some jade along with a few yaks. Slabs of jade are good to bargain with later in your travels. Yaks are sure-footed, warm to sleep with at night, and hard working. Yak milk is good to drink, yak butter good for cooking and lighting the dark. Dried yak poop is useful because you can turn it into firewood. We'll add blankets and get new gloves and hats. This is our continent's mountainous northeastern corner. With such life-saving supplies we can proceed south to Pakistan. There we'll get rid of our yaks, and furs, and ride the desert camels west, following ancient trade routes across Arabia and Yemen, where the Queen of Sheba came from, until we've made our way back to Sinai."

Whatever its differences, this continent's shared imaginations now move across the world, as they have always done across its own vast spaces, like fertile underwater currents coursing ocean depths.

* * *

In the evenings the passengers sat on the deck chairs, watching the sun balance on the horizon. It got redder and redder but did not seem to move. Then it fell suddenly behind the earth. The sea became the texture of heavy grey silk.

India was just over the horizon.

Even after the sun had gone it was too hot to go below. We would sit on in darkness, watching the stars surfacing one by one. We searched out constellations, and recognized our tippy dish-shaped galaxy. Sometimes it seemed we could see the farthest depths of the universe, like black holes in a chocolate pudding. The heavy ocean dissolved beneath us and we sailed a sea of stars. Space itself, so smoky black and impenetrable, seemed to be poked back in some places and to press forward in others. There were blacker depths to parts of he sky. Depths I could imagine and then, as my eyes moved, I couldn't imagine any longer. The deep darkness of space seemed like black dough pressed and fingered by a giant dirty hand searching for diamonds.

We told the children Jataka tales. The little Buddha stories stirred their hearts. In the stories Buddha became the Lion, the Grass, the Monkey, anything that was noble and compassionate. The tales gently confirmed the close connection the children already had with nature. They also confirmed inklings of lives larger than the children's own. Later they would help to dissolve the terrifying certainties of birth and death which would crash into their consciousness like meteors soon enough. The remembrance of rhythms infinitely grand would help to harmonize the children into the infinitely grand universe. Someday I hoped to hear them say:

"And I myself am a miniature world."

It is mind-stretching stuff, cuddled cozily together and feeling the gentle rocking of the boat beneath you, to reflect on such things. Does the universe have an end? Does it have a beginning? Can it keep expanding?

Were not the children, if all went right, expanding universes themselves? The universe seemed a reflection of their own individual states. Their little bodies would expand to a definite limit set by the locks of evolution, But their inner life, at least for the time being, was expanding without any limits in sight.

But it is no use reflecting the universe unless the world you mirror is vast enough. A world made up of atoms and space is not enough. It must have compassion, sacrifice, and laughter, too.

14. BOMBAY HARBOR

Fire Boats

The ocean calmed into a deep blue puddle. Occasionally a butterfly fluttered about the ship, circling haphazardly, reminding us of the fragrance of flowers and the almost forgotten smells of earth. The air was heavy and sweet with the scent of land.

One night as we sat bathed in the salty red air, we watched some low-slung black boats wobble past on the evening sea. At first there were only a few, but soon there were dozens. Sky and sea were red. We could see land, a black streak in the distance. The great embrace that is the Bay of Bombay stretched out to greet us.

Before long there were dozens of boats, of all sizes, silhouetted black against the last rays of sunset. On the left, brooding like a mourning figure, loomed the sacred island of Elephanta.

Suddenly a loud roar shattered the still evening.

"What's that?" Jeff wanted to know.

We went to the rail and looked over its side. Splashing water into a fountain of red colors, two anchor chains tore through the ocean's skin.

"It's the anchors," Alex said, puzzled.

"They don't want to maneuver the harbor at night?" I suggested.

"I guess that's it."

Blackness dropped with the unfamiliar suddenness of the tropics. A silver atomic reactor far away caught one last red gleam, then all was dark. We went below for dinner.

The next morning we were woken by sounds of delight from the children who were already out on deck.

"Come look, Mummy," Jeff cried into the cabin. "Fireboats! Come. Look! Eight! Ten!"

Hurrying outside, we saw where Jeff pointed.

"What's going on?" I asked.

"We're surrounded by fireboats," Alex said.

"Look how many!" Jeff exclaimed.

We climbed to our Star Deck to see what was happening. The entire crew and all the officers were on main deck, visibly nervous. Everyone had been given a position to maintain. This was unusual, because unloading was usually done by native stevedores at freighter stops. The crew, those who were not on duty or were without day-passes, took advantage of the time to sleep off their slivovic. Now sailors we had never seen before had appeared above deck to take their stations. They stood waiting for orders, taut with tension.

A string of shiny new, bright red and brass tugboats lined up beside us with large signs saying "Explosives! Danger! Keep Off!"

The excitement entranced the children, particularly the chubby red fireboats that encircled our ship, cheerfully waving and honking, checking their powerful hoses by spraying them high into the air, creating myriad small rainbows.

"So we had them after all," Alex said.

"For a dam?"

"Or a war."

"At least we're not smuggling." I tried looking on the bright side.

"No, this shipment was expected, evidently. Meanwhile," he lowered his voice: "We're getting off this crazy tub while they unload!"

"The way to go," I said.

The pudgy second mate, standing nearby, turned sharply, hands on wide hips. "You not get off until unloading be finished. Captain's orders."

"We have children!"

The mate looked nervously over his shoulder. "We no dock till tomorrow, Mister. Safer to unload cargo on Bombay barges."

"Safer for Bombay, anyway," I said.

He laughed politely.

Bjorn gallivanted up to us. Arabella, curious, hovered a few steps behind. The second mate left hurriedly.

"Explosives! I told you so! I knew it all along. My friend, the third mate, he would not lie to me! The crew say it is to build a dam in north India, but it is really ammunition for the war with Pakistan. It comes all the way from Czechoslovakia. The arms capital of the world! " He grinned at the kids, who up till then had been too interested in the goings on to listen to our conversation. Then he danced off to spread the word.

"Did you hear what Bjorn said?" Jeff asked solemnly. "Explosives. The boat might explode."

I met Alex's eyes. "What are we going to do?" I asked.

"Not much to do," Alex said. "We're eleven miles from shore!"

We watched Bjorn buzzing from one passenger to the next, spreading the alarming news. The officers tensely patrolled the loading deck.

Stefan came to explain that the ship's agent was due soon and unloading would begin once he left.

"I thought we were going to be in Bombay for ten days!" I said. "Surely we're not expected to travel eleven miles back and forth every day?"

"Tomorrow we be in dry-dock."

"Why tomorrow?"

Stefan looked upset. He spoke softly: "I am responsible for passengers."

"I'm glad you are," I said, encouragingly.

"Captain cares only for his cargo. But I am punished in Rijecka if there is any trouble with passengers."

Jane Winslow Eliot

"What sort of trouble?"

"He is good captain." Stefan leaned only slightly closer. Lowering his voice but speaking casually, without emphasis, he added: "The mail boat arrive at nine with ship's agent. If you have mail you take it to agent at nine. He take it immediately to shore in his boat." Leaning down, to drop his arms lightly around the children's shoulders, he said louder: "You come ring the gong at twelve."

I gazed after him as he disappeared down the ladder. Alex looked at me, pale and tight-lipped. We understood.

The children hopped around us, bursting with excitement.

We sensed the arrogant dismay felt by the crew as the Indians took over the unloading. A nervous Bombay native, half the size of the beefy sailor who usually manned the ship's deck-crane, now replaced him. From the bridge, the captain watched, stony-faced, as the crane clumsily began to lift off the metal hatch. The tilting iron cover banged three times as it rose, turning the ship into a malevolent gong.

Everyone jumped. Two natives threw themselves onto the deck, hands over their heads. The second mate went over to the Indian operator and tried to explain the mechanics in broken English.

I noticed a tiny white boat, its deck shaded by white canvas, bouncing toward the steep white side of the freighter. It was the mail boat Stefan had mentioned. I glanced at my watch. Ten minutes to nine.

Down in the deepest hold, chains had been fastened around a raw wood crate with a cheery red line slashed diagonally across. The crate slowly rose into the wet morning sunlight.

The first mate called out abruptly. Another officer strode over to the crane operator who was still having difficulty.

"Up, more up!" he commanded furiously. "Up!"

The crate hit the side of the hold with a reverberating thud. An Indian leapt overboard. The captain disappeared from the bridge. The Indian at the crane froze.

Alex exclaimed. "We can't just stand here!"

I glanced again at the little white boat, now pinned to the side of the freighter. Anyone inside was hidden from view by the canvas top.

Alex followed my gaze.

""We've got ten minutes," I said, in a low voice, placing my back against the railing and looking around in a slightly vague way not to alert anyone, passengers or crew. "Let's go get our mail and take it to him."

The canvas covering could hide us if we got down without being stopped.

"Okay, let's go," Alex said. "You take Wyd; I'll take Jeff. I'll get our letters on the way."

I knew he meant passports and money. He hadn't written any letters.

"I'll go starboard with Wyd, you go port with Jeff. Walk slow," I said softly.

Alex barely nodded. No accidental body language.

I took Wyd's hand, walking around the deck once. I got her to chant a poem as we went downstairs. So long as no one caught suspicion from any odd movement, we might not be stopped. We had to outwit people who knew the hidden gestures of suspicion, fear, and rebellion. Since childhood it had sometimes meant their lives.

Wyd and I went below by the inside stairway. We talked about what she would write in her book. I let her describe the pictures she planned to draw. We met no one until we saw Stefan shadowed in a doorway on the lower deck that led to the gangplank. As soon as he had seen us, he disappeared without a sign.

We edged down the unguarded gangplank, keeping close to the ship's side. The tiny motor launch was empty. A quick jump and we were aboard. Wyd looked surprised but entirely confident. My heart pounded to the crash of metal against metal as the sloppy unloading continued.

A few minutes after I began to get nervous, Alex arrived with Jeff. We settled in silence and waited, grateful for the white canvas that sheltered us from curious eyes.

The agent joined us. After his initial astonishment, he smiled his understanding: "You do not want to stay on this boat with children!"

Without waiting, he revved his motor. The launch pushed off. The sleek white illusion shrank behind us, at least for a little while.

15. ELEPHANTA

Sacred Lingams

It took over an hour to reach land and another in a tiny tin-roofed building to clear passport control, although we were the only ones there. It had to do with a bottle of scotch we thought we could bring in. It precipitated a torrent of talk, about an hour's worth, which we could not follow, and during that time a person from the ship arrived to watch the proceedings. Finally, we were made to understand that India was a totally dry country and not even one bottle of liquor could enter. We left it on the Custom Master's desk, and were immediately free to take a black, high-roofed taxi to a hotel which he assured us was the best in town. I settled back into the deep, red-velvet seat, Wyd beside me. Alex sat on one red velvet jump seat, Jeff on the other. The driver suggested we pull down the blinds, it being so hot. But we were eager to see everything.

The main thoroughfare from the harbor was densely crowded with people.

"Where is everybody going?" Jeff asked, gazing out.

As we made our slow way around hand-pulled carts, bicycles, trucks, cars, and people, it became clear that the pedestrians were not going anywhere. They were living on the sidewalks. Some had set up beds, some had even managed lean-tos against a wall. If they weren't doing anything else, the sidewalk citizens simply stared straight ahead, arms constantly dancing about their bodies, scratching. A little boy pee'd into the gutter. Garbage, piled high on a street corner, was being picked over by a small crowd. The car swerved around a horse-drawn cart, then slowed for a motor scooter. We saw five women kneeling over a dead body stretched out on the pavement. Nearby, another woman washed a dress in the gutter. All the way along children sat, feet in the small trickle of fluid that was running down the side of each street. A man filled a cooking pan from the same source. Our driver skillfully maneuvered the car past another wagon. Pulled by two men, it was piled high with coffins.

"They pick up the dead from the street," the driver explained. "Usually they go at night, but when it is hot, they go in day too."

Wyd clung to my hand. I tried to shield the children from seeing the street by talking to them, but I was too shattered by the sights to be successful. Papers twirled across the road, blown by traffic, but were immediately caught by an adolescent as more than precious. A small boy stood looking vacantly at the passers-by, his stomach distended, his arms and legs like pins. A little girl lay on the sidewalk, her legs twitching feebly. An old man turned his back and crapped into the gutter. The car slowed as three ragged young women hobbled across the street, their thin legs running sores. Each tenderly carried a dirty cloth which wrapped a baby. A family knelt around a fire, cooking a small rodent, the men determinedly defending their meal from a circle of outsiders.

Suddenly making a sharp turn, our taxi moved into another world. Down a few streets we could see the ocean. On one side of the street was a wide, sandy beach with a clean walkway necklacing the expansive curve it carved up the coast. Waves curled in clean, sparkling coolness. On the other side of the quiet, wide road, flowers grew in elegant exuberance in gardens carefully tended under shady plane trees. Chauffeur-driven cars cruised in stately fashion, white apartment houses, and grand hotels gleamed graciously in the sun. The Indians here were well-dressed, the men in western-style suits, the women with flowing silk saris catching slight breezes and making delicate patterns in the sweet-smelling air.

Turning off the beachfront, we were soon deposited at the hotel. It was a grand wooden structure, in Victorian gingerbread style. A thin, old man showed us to our rooms. Adjoining, they were extraordinarily large, with high ceilings. In each room were two wide beds, shrouded with ghostly mosquito nets hanging over them from a brass ring attached to the ceiling. Dark wood floors stretched away to tall shutters, which opened onto a shared balcony. The old man turned on an enormous wooden ceiling fan that slowly began to stir the humid air. It was not even remotely cool.

Jeff and Wyd bounced gleefully on their beds, hauling down mosquito nets in the process. Alex and I went into the other room. He opened the terrace shutters, letting bright heat crash onto the floor. Feeling sticky and dirty, I went looking for the shower that was down the hall.

Emerging a bit refreshed, I found Alex had ordered bottles of mineral water for us all. The ice in the ice-bucket had already melted but he poured us glassfuls which I drank gratefully.

We talked over what we should do about going on with our trip. Alex suggested we talk to someone at the American embassy and ask for advice. But I was reluctant. I didn't want to tangle with the mechanisms of American bureaucracy.

"They'll probably advise us to get off the ship," I said. "And they may be within their rights to refuse to let us continue, because of the war in southeast Asia. We don't have the money to go on some other way or to go back."

"At least now they'll have gotten rid of the explosives. It explains the captain's paranoia all this time. He was terrified we'd mention them to the authorities. We wouldn't have been able to go through the Suez, or to bunker at Aden. Maybe he'll be more relaxed now that they've been off-loaded."

But we didn't really know what we should do. I felt an unfamiliar longing for roots in familiar soil.

"This afternoon let's visit the sacred island of Elephanta," Alex suggested. "And tomorrow we'll make arrangements to fly to the sacred caves of Ajanta and Ellora."

"That sounds good. And first let's find a cool place for lunch."

Jeff and Wyd scampered along the balcony we shared, bubbling with laughter. They were thrilled to be on land again.

That afternoon we took a boatman's holiday and putted out by motor launch to the small island of Elephanta, which sat meditating in the still waters of the larger Bay of Bombay. Guided by a thoughtful young monk, we wandered the dusty pathways that wound under enormous trees twirled about with tenacious yellow vines. The trail led inevitably into the darkness of the temple, which in turn was a dusty labyrinth of corridors leading to a central, open space. It stood empty but for a lingam, a phallic, stone object about four feet tall, covered in fresh pink and yellow flowers.

We stayed, mystified yet awed, for some time. I tried to imagine what this unprepossessing stone altar could mean to me. Were real powers flowing through the stone? Was I able to feel them? Or was it just to remind me of something, like a postcard from a beach resort? The flowers were wilting in the heat. Was it power by analogy, a message to say that spiritual power, which you don't know, is like sexual power, which you do? I could not concentrate. Without enough to distract me, images of the morning's frightful taxi ride invaded my brain.

At last the monk led us out to the entrance. We blinked, dazzled by the hot afternoon sunlight. Above the neighboring islands, to our total amazement, rose another lingam, skyscraper high! Silver in color, it fiercely flashed in the late afternoon sun's red rays.

"What's that?" I asked with a shudder.

Raising his curiously curved yellow cane, the monk pointed: "That's an atomic reactor," he murmured softly. "A gift from you, to help against our poverty."

"I don't think that's the best of American largesse," Alex said.

113

The priest, who had been mostly quiet until then, laughed out loud: "It worries you, I see. It worries us, also."

"Today," I said, feeling our host would understand, "I realized something for the first time. I saw something about money. It does not flow naturally like water. I thought it did. I was told it did. I thought it naturally flowed down and around. But today I see it goes just so far, then it rebounds into a corner where it stacks up. I can see this happening to America, as it already has to India."

"Ah, it must all change."

"Is there the will?

"You understand." His dark eyes seemed to be looking just over my shoulder at horizons far beyond my own. "Today we too are afraid because of the sleep of the soul."

"People follow leaders, and I don't want to. Any. But I don't want to lead either."

"You are too soon."

"If everyone had to take the ride from Bombay harbor to the center of town, wouldn't we have a new world?"

"Well, you see," he bowed his head, his voice gentle, "When our friends in Washington make us a gift of that, you see," he pointed to the silver building, "we knew we had to make a gift of the same importance. Before we are ready, you see. It is so much they give away. They do not see it is upside down. So the sages at the source of the Ganges – they do not speak, even to each other – they see it is a special moment in all history. They communicate with other wise men, who are lesser because they speak. The lesser sages tell us to send a gift back to the Americans. Most important, a matter of life and death. But what can we give? Americans have great power, but they are like children of ten years. They play friendly with dangerous toys."

Meanwhile, Alex was fascinated by the monk's cane. It spiraled up in thick and sturdy curves. "May I see it?" he asked.

The monk handed it to him. "It is to befuddle the devils," he explained. "They do not know if you come or if you go."

"It's amazing."

The monk refused to take it back. "It is my gift to you," he said.

* * *

"It was melted butter in Bombay," Wyd wrote later in her book. "We went to the aquarium to see some things that swam under the Jessenice. We slept under mosquito nets because of the mosquitoes."

That night, after the children were in bed, Alex and I took two chairs onto the balcony. The huge night sky encompassed us like a heavy porcelain bowl. Night had brought no relief from the heat. As we sipped warmish mineral water, we heard he children talking quietly.

"It feels funny being off the ship, doesn't it?"

"Yes."

"Nothing rocks. And it's so noisy."

"Look at the patterns the lights from the street make on the ceiling," Jeff said after a moment.

"Okay."

"It looks like a man with a hat on if you look at him one way. Or a field with a highway going through it if you look at it from the side. Let's count how many things we see."

"I don't see the man. I see a bear with his paw stretched out."

"Oh, right. That's better, really. I saw his nose as being the man's shoulder."

"I get it. And I can see a skyscraper."

"How many things is that?" He counted off the shadowy images they had seen and added: "I see a window with curtains. But does that count? Because it's really the light coming through the window."

"We'll count everything," Wyd replied loyally.

We heard them get up to twenty-four things before they drifted off to sleep. Alex refilled our glasses.

"It's hard to get used to being off the boat."

"I know. I feel as though everything's still moving."

I didn't think I'd ever get to sleep that night. I could not get used to the solidity beneath us. Alex felt the same way. We sat out on the balcony, drinking mineral water and talking till dawn.

16. ELLORA AND AJANTA

Sacred Caves

I nstead of going to the American embassy the next morning we went to a travel agent.

"You arrive in the cool season," the agent smiled, mopping his brow in the oven hot breeze that dropped from a giant fan attached to the ceiling. The thermometer registered 104 degrees. "You are fortunate not to require air-conditioning."

After the arrangements were made we went into the sunbleached Bombay streets to do some exploring. It turned out to be a depressing plan. Poverty and disease pervaded everything.

"Why don't they do something?" I said. "Why don't they all join hands and march into the main square and refuse to take it any more?"

"I know what you mean," Alex responded. "But that's what they're finally doing in Indonesia. Trouble is, it usually means war."

We decided to go early to the airport.

"Even the captain can't help but be affected by all this," I said. "You'll see. Everyone will rush into each other's arms when we're back on the boat. They must realize that we simply have to be kind to each other, or look what will happen?"

"You'd think everyone would wake up when they saw this," Alex agreed.

Before long we found ourselves on a twelve-passenger plane, buzzing low over ginger-brown earth and chocolate-brown rivers on our way to Aurangabad, the airport destination on the way to the sacred caves. Squares of saffron yellow and dark poinsettia-red relieved the dusky immensity. In some countries it is the sky that tells of eternity. In India it is the land. There seems to be no end to the fruitful earth laced inexplicably with hunger and despair.

The children were delighted to be on a small airplane.

"Why don't the wings go up and down?" asked Wyd.

"Why is it so loud?" asked Jeff. "Why is earth tipping? It doesn't on the boat."

Aurangabad Airport, our immediate destination, was a small rectangle of grey in the huge patchwork quilt of farms and villages that stretched hot and flat as far as the eyes could see. From there an ancient taxi, bumping and rattling loudly, steered us for what seemed like hours, under what felt like fire, through a mix of people, bicycles, cattle-drawn carts, and ancient cars to our hotel, a large wooden relic of British colonial rule. A tall Sikh houseboy, dressed in blue and white silk, with a large turban wrapped around his head and a long silk sash around his middle, lay across the stairs to the bedrooms. Dozing in his uncomfortable spot, he held onto a shiny kriss – a naked, curved sword about two feet long if ever straightened. We stepped over him carefully, hoping his dreams would register that we were not enemy intruders but duly registered guests.

Our two large rooms were cool and dark, with the usual thick, dusty mosquito nets draped over enormous four-poster beds. We stretched out for ten minutes, then thirst won over rest and we went downstairs and out onto the hotel's huge verandah-dining room for lunch. There were only two other guests in the vast expanse of wicker chairs and tables, an Indian couple sitting in silence as the man read his newspaper. His wife seemed to be searching the horizon for something she'd lost. Selecting a large round table, we sat in outsized chairs amid a great deal of greenery, and ordered iced ginger ale and iced-tea from a very upright and silent waiter. A few minutes later, a young, well-dressed Britisher slumped silently into an armchair nearby and despondently prepared to watch the horizon, pretend to read the newspaper, and listen to our conversation. Rattling a large bucket of fast-melting ice, our waiter reappeared to also serve our drinks. He explained the plan for tomorrow. A car would take us to the sacred caves of Ellora, about an hour's drive away. We would be given a picnic so we could stay there all day.

The children quietly wrote in their books.

In the enormous distance, after some time, a large group of Indians appeared on the dusty, straight road in front of the hotel, driving a herd of oxen. As they slowly came nearer we could make out their colorful costumes, their listless, languid walk, their variety of animal, donkeys, cattle, dogs; as well as babies, children, husbands, and helpers. They flowed in a gold and rust colored cloud of dust, in one slow motion, as a group, as much a part of the burning pavement, the richly colored air, and the dark red sunset, as they were part of their softly-tinted, body-shrouding, filmy garments. We watched, it seemed forever, as they approached along the road that curved in front of our gingerbread hotel. Their sibilant, chattering voices carried up to our cool verandah, growing louder as they neared, then passed and gradually faded. We heard them long after they had disappeared around a long bend in the road.

All of us stayed quiet in the rising stillness, watching as a sun bigger than any we had ever seen, descended, pulsing, into hot, dark dust. It seemed to be the very heart of the eternal continent, splashing spectacular contortions of ochre and purples across the vast Indian sky around and above us. The dust of the land held the vivid reds longest, then, suddenly it all vanished into black. Black is the true color of the Indian continent. I do not think I have ever seen black so clean, clear, transparent, secretive, or vast in all my travels.

The driver who took us to Ellora the following morning turned out to be the same cheery fellow who had picked us up at the airport. His car had lost a back door overnight. It still rattled and zigzagged at high speed through the tapestry of traffic.

On the highway, sometimes right in the center of it, were people and people with other cars, and people with carts, with oxen, and more people. People just standing, waiting, looking, talking, but mostly just waiting.

"What are they waiting for?" Jeff wanted to know as we swerved around a man standing patiently in the middle of the road.

We shrugged helplessly. Waiting for nothing. It was not going to get any cooler, and nobody was coming to help.

By the time we arrived at the sacred site it was the hottest part of the day. The car stopped in a grove of trees. Wild monkeys chattered overhead and called their young to look at the funny people. Alex called our young to look back.

There are about twenty-eight sacred caves, side by side, at Ellora, mostly single rectangles, but some have two stories and a many as four rooms. They are intricately carved into the cliffs, with grandiose tales of gods and heroes. Our monk-guide turned on the electric lights in the first cave, but quickly turned them off again in response to Alex's appalled reaction to the distortion of colors and shapes of frescoes that had been created long before the invention of electric lights.

Inside and out, the stone had been carved to depict scenes from the sacred tales of the Hindus. One dancing figure had five arms and legs, all in rhythmic harmony. Jeff preferred the god with ten arms. The children caught the lilt of his dance and imitated it, laughing together. Our kindly guide smiled appreciatively.

"The air in this cave is carved out of living rock," I told the kids.

Jeff was annoyed by this image.

"I mean that it's not a cave in the usual sense of the word," I explained. "More like a hand-hewn place of meditation, dug into the cliffs, rather than out of them. If the architects wanted a column, they just carved around the stone, leaving an untouched pillar of rock still standing."

119

At sunset we returned to the cool of our hotel verandah, hot and exhausted. As fascinating as they were, the caves and their sculptures had not penetrated through the turbulence of our emotions.

"I was hoping for something different," Alex confessed over dinner. "A real experience. This felt too much like history."

"Ajanta may be different," I said hopefully.

Alex looked at me. "Yes, let's do better there."

We left the hotel in the cool of the very early morning. The expedition started badly. The children quarrelling; Alex morose. I fell more and more into myself, churning. The very picturesque-ness of the ancient black taxi, rather like a large Egyptian sarcophagus on wheels, shrouded us in gloom.

We were the first to arrive at Ajanta, besides the ticket collector. A narrow earthen path some eight to ten stories high led almost straight up to the thirty or so caves. These lay side by side in an enormous arc high upon the face of a sheer cliff, at the end of the large horseshoe canyon. A thin pipe railing edged the precipice. We stepped gingerly, holding onto the children so they could not slip off without us. Like eagles, we looked down on the river rushing through the canyon below.

Heat increased as we climbed. Sweating and puffing, we reached the slender, fairly flat crescent running along outside the cave entrances. I was still churning like a sea in storm. Alex wanted to go slowly. Hot and irritated, I moved slightly faster, looking for a dark, cool cave, leaving him with the children.

"The frescoes here are over a thousand years old," I heard him explain.

"Who painted them?" Jeff asked.

"Buddhist monks. They ground up stones to make their colors. Maybe later we can pick up some to take back to the boat, and see if we can make them, too."

"It must have been lovely when all those monks were walking around in those yellow robes," Wyd said dreamily.

"They were probably sleeping if it was this hot," Jeff said.

I walked on, out of earshot. By now a busload of Japanese had arrived. Sticking close together, they dutifully trudged in and out of caves. Soon there were busloads from other nations, as well, with guides spouting facts in half a dozen languages. Such fast-paced tourism made a mockery of pilgrimage.

I hurried on until I was far from family, guards, guides, and tours. I was forever doing that, I realized, as I paused to gaze straight down to the brown river far below. I was forever trying to leave people out, as I had the cut-out paper dolls I used to play with as a child. The form that remained, made purely of air in the sheets of cardboard, were always more appealing, more real, than the dolls themselves.

Climbing over a large pile of cement rock and splintered wood at the far end of the arc, I found a cave with no guard, no electric light, no visitors, and no chance anyone but me might climb over the dangerous debris to get inside. Centuries before, the cave had been left unfinished, and, fortunately current tastes still left intact its unembellished beauty. I stood at the entrance. The craftsmen's working methods showed clearly in the slanting rays of the morning sun. Here, too, the monks had hollowed the space starting from top down, but had seldom reached the bottom. Cautiously, I walked inside. The bottom half of the cave had remained untouched, as if awaiting someone to finish the vision – perhaps by bringing the ceiling closer to my head, and putting at eye level carvings meant to be seen high up on the walls. This cave had waited for centuries for someone to carve emptiness all the way down to its still hidden floor. No one had done so. Looking down, I felt the presence of shapes buried in stone, imagined but never laid bare.

It was like seeing that one had a destiny.

As my eyes adjusted to the darkness deep inside, I began to make out two figures which had been sculpted in high-relief, almost in round. They, too, seemed to have been discovered rather than created. One was a reclining Buddha stretching the entire wall to my left. Further in was a large panel so clearly carved that, even in the gloom, every detail stood out.

It was an odd composition for these caves. Buddha was sitting cross-legged in the center of a smooth, empty almond of space. Encircling this silent area was a giant wreath picturing all manner of temptations. Naked girls sang and danced for him, naked youths brandished swords and books. Others passed with wine cups held high, listening to music-makers. Here was the beautiful world designed to distract any young prince from his meditations, to agitate his self-control, to buzz-saw through his silence like a neighbor's grass-cutting machine. Exquisite figures, graceful and harmless, vied for his attention. His all-seeing eyes remained serene. The pageant twirled and twined around him, gaining in frenzy as I filled it with my own imaginings.

Buddha sat in his silent, empty center, unmoved.

For a moment I saw the empty spaces of the cut-out dolls I had filled so solemnly in my youth. I had been yearning to see the unfinished stuff of my future. But I was distracted even as I watched. My center was an amorphous, undirected commotion, vulnerable to each passing play, mere opaque longing and confusion, prey to all promises and proposals. I was definitely pressed and scratched by the prickly wreath of wondrous temptations encircling me.

How could it be otherwise, I thought with a dull ache. Education had not led me inward as I was trying to lead the children. I had not been taught how to create a still center within myself, to strengthen it, to make it grow, so that it would withstand all onslaught. I had not been shown how to pull the prickly wreath of life around myself in such a way as to remain unpricked by it. Worse, I had been taught that all the excitement of the prickly wreath was the real me.

I gazed at the half-closed eyes of the Buddha.

Buddha maintained his serenity in the face of the beautiful world. But it was the ugliness of the world that awakened his compassion and brought him back.

The ugliness. That was the hardest part. Like a poor country peasant in the jungle of the city, I was lost in unfamiliar regions. There were no familiar sounds of the night. There were no stars to guide me. I was not a slum child when I began. I became so.

A slum child of the spirit.

How did it happen?

There was something in this cave. Something was in the stillness that surrounded the sitting Buddha; something that held at bay the thorny wreath of life that pricked at it. The narrow ellipse of empty stone around him began to overshadow everything else.

I could never be that still.

I gazed at the carving.

Perhaps I could.

Perhaps the narrow almond of smooth stone was the place to start. It might give me protection and room. Protection from the prickles and distraction of the outer world. Room to turn inward.

As I stood gazing at the perfect stillness of the compassionate figure in the center of his know-it-all world, I felt the delicate loosening of bonds too tight.

Stillness could shield me from the overflowing junkyard of criticism and applause. Stillness could help me realize specific dreams, not confused, vague ones.

Stillness could protect me from myself.

* * *

The children and Alex silhouetted themselves against the blinding sunlight at the cave entrance. It was noon, the time of day when caves were blackest.

I beckoned them in to share the Garlanded Buddha with me.

"The Buddha," I said, "was a prince when he was young. He lived in a palace covered with fragrant flowers. No dust or dirt or awful smells ever reached him; flowers filtered all away. Sun never burnt him, rain never got him wet. Beauty shielded him. Until one day he saw sickness, suffering and death. Like we did this morning. Then he sat down under a tree. 'I shall wait right here,' he said, 'Until I know.'"

"Know what?" asked Jeff.

"Know anything. Anything at all. And he did. He waited in silence under the bee-humming Bodhi Tree until he knew something."

"What did he know?" Jeff persisted.

"He knew he could reach stillness. He knew he could disappear into the stillness and be at peace forever. But instead, he turned around. He came back into our world to help others find this peace, stillness, emptiness."

My new kind of cut-outs.

"It was a momentous discovery that he could share with everyone. He wanted to help people. He taught them how to help each other. Then some of them came up here and carved these caves. They wanted to live together in a peaceful group. To help each other and try to learn something too. They made the caves beautiful to match."

"Match what?" Wyd asked.

"Match the flowers, and the river, and the sun, and things. They all learned how to reach the stillness."

Together we walked back along the path and down the immense cliff of stairs crudely hacked out by the monks hundreds of years before. Then holding hands, we edged our way along the dangerous crescent top. Occasionally looking over the frail railing, we saw the river way below, and beside it, alone, unattended, a tiny tea-house. Grasping the rickety railing, we navigated the rough cliff-side down past the up-trudging tours, past the wild monkeys, down through the valley's mind-stunning midday heat, until we reached the tiny blue and white tile tea-house which stood beside the cool river, gurgling along the very bottom of the canyon. Its roof was made of many-colored bougainvillea, dotted with the tiny red trumpets of a flame vine. Three flowery archways let in fragrant air while keeping out the heat. There were four wide wooden benches, all empty. No one had yet ventured this far down.

Gratefully, we opened the surprising treats in the picnic basket that our hotel had provided.

Afterwards, we stretched out contentedly, each on a bench, gazing up at the flowery roof. Purple and red blossoms dreamed overhead. Occasionally Wyd's fingers followed the movements of a bit of flame vine over her head.

After a while we were joined by an Indian family as small as ours. Squeezing onto two benches in order to make room for the others, we lay companionably and listened in silence to the immense stillness of the land. Nothing stirred but the billion-year old hum of insects. Sun, bees, and fragrances kneaded our stillness.

At long last the sun stretched its shadow veil across us. We stretched, too, and stood up, bowed to our karmic friends, and retraced the stairs leading to the parking lot. The driver honked us over to his antique vehicle. He had fixed the door. The sun was near the horizon as we drove home. Its light glowed garnet. The very air was crimson. Palm trees, oxen, and wandering people were jet black against the vast blood-red color. The horizon seemed to be above eye level. Suddenly the sun disappeared, leaving its pulsating redness flattened across the western sky. We drove in fast falling darkness, along the black ribbon of road, swerving dangerously around black objects in our unlit path.

When the red vanished everything turned deepest black.

The driver did not put out his lights.

"I can see just as well in the dark when my eyes get used to it," he explained, reassuringly.

"Do you suppose he was blind all along?" Alex whispered in my ear.

* * *

Several days later, back in Bombay, a different taxi swerved us down a steep, unfamiliar road and left us off in the middle of the afternoon turmoil of a working dock. We could not see our ghostly ship or even the harbor. Just piles of soot, bags of scrap metal, rusting paraphernalia.

"Follow there to find your ship," the taxi driver pointed helpfully to a black oblong shadow.

We picked our way around pyramids of coal and cubes of pressed scrap metal, over fallen wood and pieces of steel cable. Through open doors, the deep black space of half-empty warehouses added darkness to the day. Coal-dust mingled with shadows of dark men, making them seem transparent as they appeared and disappeared into rectangles of black air. Fallen oblongs of pale transparent yellow sunlight draped themselves over black sacks and stacks of rags and garbage, revealing nothing.

Soon we came to some stairs that led further down. A turn in their direction, and we were at eye level with Jessenice's top-most deck. She was floating in a sort of pond surrounded by walls. We had forgotten dry-dock. Soot had settled gently over her like a mourning veil.

"Sinister looking, isn't she?" Alex said. "And yet there's something reassuring about her. Why's that?"

"Familiarity, maybe?"

Our freighter was the only familiar object in the blackened chaos of the docks.

Alex held out his hands to Jeff and Wyd as we took the steps that led down to the ship's passenger deck and the gangplank. Then he held out his hand to me to jump aboard. Alex always offered a feeling that all was as it should be.

At dinner, the passengers were curious to know where we had been.

"We were allowed off only from nine until six each day," Harold said in annoyance.

"Yes, I'm sure we all would have liked to visit those caves," added Arabella. "It doesn't seem fair that you got off."

Stefan came in and told Alex the captain wanted to see him.

When he'd left, Arabella said to me: "Captain Stanislav is very upset that you left the ship without telling him. Bjorn says he threatened to shoot Stefan if it happened again. Although what Stefan had to do with it, beats me."

"Me too," I said.

Alex was gone for less than twenty minutes. When he returned to the lounge, I asked: "What did he want?"

"Whooosh! To give me holy hell. And to get our passports. I declined to give them to him."

"And?"

Alex sipped from a glass of slivovic Stefan brought in without being asked.

"He was apoplectic. By the way, I just want to say, you were a genius to get our passports stamped with visas for every port, not just every country. It made all the difference."

"How come?"

"He thought he might have to sail without us. In which case he would have been held responsible for 'losing' part of his 'cargo,' as he insists on calling us. I assured him that if we'd missed the ship we would have flown to its next port-of-call, Madras, and re-joined the boat all there. With our visas, that would have been no problem. So he calmed down a bit at the end."

"I'm glad you spoke to him, not me," I said, wishing I could "whoosh" as satisfactorily as Alex was able to.

Alex laughed at the thought of our captain having to confront an irritated Jane.

"For his sake, I am too," he said.

* * *

At four o'clock next morning, I awoke suddenly to an unfamiliar sound and went out on deck in the dark. The Jessenice had started up and was once more on its ghostly way. Stars were obscured. Only a thin necklace of yellow glimmered weakly along the water's edge. I went right back down to wake Alex and the kids. Once again there was something new to be seen from our floating perch. The Jessenice was about to pass through a lock.

Sleepily, we took positions so we could overlook the prow. The ship was gliding slowly toward massive iron gates. With dreamlike heaviness they silently opened, welcoming the ship to a space just a bit larger than itself. A torrent of water poured in both front and back of us, gently heaving our vessel some thirty feet higher up.

We passed through two more locks in this way, and by dawn we were back at sea level, narrowly banked in on either side. A few native stevedores stood waiting on the banks. Five of our crewmen appeared on the cargo deck below. Stooping, they attached thin lead-lines to the thick rope-coils which lay ready there. Then with no more than a low grunt or two, our sailors hoisted the heavy rope-coils over their shoulders. Gracefully tossing the lead-lines to the stevedores on shore, they then spun lightly around on the balls of their feet to hurl the coils themselves! The Indian stevedores hauled in their ropes by the lead-lines. Then, without missing a beat, they turned as one and, incredibly, began to pull our ship, without knotting the ropes to anything but themselves. Their burden was lightened only slightly by minimal momentum from the ship, but it was they who, bent and sweating, kept it from crashing against the sides of the channel as they eased their mighty burden through.

Motors thumped. The Indian stevedores tossed back our lines. We shouted bravos to such legendary people – men who could pull a freighter.

They waved back as our shadowy ship slipped smoothly away into the sunrise and the welcome salty, blue freshness of the ocean.

17. MOUTH OF THE INDUS

New Passengers

"Stefan, take this gunk away!" We were seated at our table for lunch as everyone was, except for the East German couple, who spent more time in their cabin than with the rest of us. Alex held up our pitcher of water for Stefan. The water was brown.

"We load water in Bombay, mister. It not settled, but it be good."

"Not for the children or Jane, Stefan." Alex's voice was quiet but firm.

Stefan lowered his voice: "You take lunch in cabin. I bring water."

He took the pitcher, covered it with his napkin, and hurried into his pantry.

We had lunch in our cabins as long as the seas were rough. For each meal, Stefan brought us clear, clean water. "The officers drink," he reassured us. "Left over from Rijecka."

The other passengers trustfully downed the brown water from Bombay, which in turn downed them. Soon everyone was having their meals, or vice versa, in their cabins. The dining room stood empty for a while. Sounds of muffled groans emanated from most cabins, but not from ours.

As we headed north, the sea became too rough for the children to go out on deck alone. Alex kept us entertained by telling more Jataka Tales – kindly animal stories about the life-thought of the Buddha's previous lives and sacrifices:

"The life that was to become the Buddha once took shape as a Chameleon, a little lizard of the kind that can change its own colors at will. He occupied the branches of his good friend, the proud and lofty Wishing Tree. One day, the King's foresters came into the woods and marked the Wishing Tree for harvesting. The King wanted timber to construct another pleasure-vessel to sail the Ganges River.

"That night word went around the forest that the Wishing Tree would be cut down and made into a ship. Many of his friends came to say goodbye. Then the Chameleon had an idea. With the Tree's permission, he burrowed in under its bark and made a hollow place underneath the foresters' mark. Next day, they returned with axes in hand. The Head Forester tapped the tree-trunk to make sure it was strong. It echoed hollowly. 'You should be more careful when you mark a tree,' he said. 'This one is rotten.' So the Wishing Tree escaped their axes.

'A little friend can be a very important friend.' That's what the leaves of the Wishing Tree whispered to the wind."

The children sighed happily.

"The Buddha used to tell this tale himself," Alex added. 'My friend Ananda was the Wishing Tree,' he would say, 'And I myself was the Chameleon.'"

The children mused in silence. After a while Jeff objected: "Buddha tells the story and takes the best part for himself. He's proud and vain."

"That's not really how it is," I said after thinking it over. "When you do something good or kind it is the goodness in you that is active. Some people call this Buddha. Others call it other names."

The children digested in silence.

"The story reminds me of the Mouse and the Lion," Wyd said.

Jeff got to his feet, and pulled Wyd to hers. "I still think he's proud and vain." They went to find Stefan for lunch. As they skipped down the corridor I heard chanting:

"I myself am the flying fish."

"I myself am the sea-gull."

"And I myself am the Buddha."

Some days later the ship docked near the entrance to the long, narrow harbor of Karachi. An icy wind swept down from the gleaming white walls of granite and ice rising to our north: the high Himalayas. The highest mountains in the world and, perhaps, one of its ten most awesome wonders, too. At night, a bright moon turned the sky black and the mountains silver. Then there seemed to be a magnetic tug of war between the mountains and the moon. We felt it coursing through us.

Camels gazed benignly from the docks, chewing in a way that reminded me of my grandmother. The dirty, cold beaches were crowded with squatters. Rows of tiny pink motorized sampans, more like tricycles than motor cars, dripped gaudy, colored chunks of glass, old beads, and paper decorations as they waited cheerfully to take us to the city some seven miles away. We bundled up in all our winter clothes and squeezed into two of them each, Wyd with Alex, Jeff with me, all huggling into the unknown.

Each morning we went into the city. We searched out odd restaurants and wandered the bazaar. There was something two dimensional about Karachi, like a mock-up for an old movie. One day we went riding on an elephant. Once we went shopping. We bought an exquisitely cut paper Christmas tree, just two feet high.

Christmas was just two weeks away.

Once we found an old man with a long white beard, sitting cross-legged at a far corner of the market. Clutching his pea-pipe, he blew musically, whereupon a cobra arose from the straw basket in front of him, slithered out, and danced for us. We were excited and apprehensive at the same time.

"It's okay," Alex assured us. "Cobra's poison has been milked. He's quite safe."

We were disappointed.

"How many times has a cobra danced for you?" I asked.

"Never before," Alex said. "I just didn't want you to be scared."

We cheered up. We had the thrill of danger, although we wondered if it really counted since there was no danger.

The cobra went on dancing, indifferently.

The evening before departure, we went out on deck. A cold blast of wind swept down from the Himalayas. Gold and fire danced their separations and their togetherness, then night dropped down like the lid of a coffin. Tiny pinpricks of starlight scratched the surface of the thin black sky.

My thoughts trailed the images of dusty Karachi, images that had not been entirely reached. There was something about the place that made me feel like a blind person who knows that something behind each touch or sound remains forever hidden. In this case it was not lost behind a veil of darkness but by a peculiar instinct. Impressions made on my senses when we were in town seemed unattached and insubstantial when we were back on board. Everything seemed to fuzz over as soon as I turned away.

Leaning over the railing, bundled against the bitter cold, we watched loading on the forward deck. Deck cargo they call it. Large piles of Spanish onions and mountains of rusty scrap iron were loaded onto deck aft. Iron covers clanged shut.

Finally we went below to bed. Alex and I had almost drifted off to sleep when, unexpectedly, laughter drifted over us, around us, cacophonous and inane.

Wonderful.

"Do you hear that?" Alex murmured. "The new passengers."

"They sound normal, positively human, even cheerful," I wondered.

"As if they got on the wrong boat," he said.

At last there were shout of "see you tomorrow," followed by more gales of laughter, and then silence.

The next morning we were up early to watch our departure from Karachi. The newcomers joined us a little later, looking friendly and hung-over. They were an open-faced, ebullient couple: "I'm Robin and this is Sallie Taylor. And this is our Andy."

They pushed forward a boy Jeff's age and size to shake hands.

"We're sorry about last night," Robin said. "I hope we didn't disturb you."

"Disturb us? It was pure heaven! We hope you have a party every night!"

"Not a common occurrence, I gather?" Robin laughed.

"Not an occurrence at all!"

"What happened was, the captain took our passports and wouldn't give them back. We couldn't get off. We sneaked a message to our friend who's the Karachi harbor pilot. We were planning to see him before we left. So he came here instead."

"The captain must have been sorry when he saw who it was," Alex grinned.

"Yes, he needs to stay on the right side of those people," Robin chuckled again.

Robin had been a forester back in England. "But we're Australians now. We have the only house on a beach with waves the size of houses. We catch everything we need and no one's around to crowd us any longer."

"I know what you mean," I said. "We used to go swimming at Marathon when we lived in Greece and there would be no one up and down the sand for at least three miles."

"Oh, it's grand all right," Robin said earnestly. "I step out of my house – I built it myself – and there's no one on that coast for three hundred miles."

I had to agree that was grander.

"I do like Harold," Arabella interrupted, materializing beside me. "Just as a friend, mind you." She took my arm and led me along the deck. "Given the opportunity, a different set of circumstances," she rambled on, "I think something might have happened between us. I really do. I'm crazy about England, you know. Always have been. Harold appreciates that."

"But you never liked damp weather," I said, taking as much interest as I could.

"Oh, that doesn't matter! The cold won't bother me if I have someone to cuddle up to." She giggled. "Bjorn doesn't interest me the same way. I don't trust him. Do you? I'm sure half the things he says are untrue."

"And half are true," I said. "I have no idea which is which."

Harold strolled over. Arabella turned her full force of her charm on him. Like a spotlight, it swept over him, pinning him. I wandered off. I passed Bjorn whispering to Bertha in the hall. I was about to join Alex and the newcomers again when I realized that Bertha had followed me. She was blotting her eyes with a handkerchief.

"Excuse me – I thought 'Arry was in 'ere –"

"Are you all right?" I put an arm around her shoulders. "Is there anything I can do?"

Bertha shook her head.

I hesitated: "Bjorn is an awful gossip, dear. You really shouldn't believe everything he says."

"I know. But I can't seem to 'elp myself. That creature's flirting with 'Arry again." She blew her nose. "I shouldn't mind like this. I want 'im to be 'appy. But he can't be any more, because of Alfie."

She blew her nose again.

"I don't know what Bjorn's been saying," I said, "but it's obvious that Harold is devoted to you."

Bertha gave a watery smile. "Yes, I know. 'Arry's a good chap. 'E'll stick it out."

"Of course he will."

"Seems funny now," Bertha went on. "We always wanted to go on a trip like this. We planned it for years, but couldn't afford it or else something would come up. Now that we're actually doing it, it's not the same. It's too late, really. We're too old."

"No, no," I protested. "It's not that. It's just a very queer ship."

"It's true, love. We both miss our 'ouse too much, an' our Alfie, you know. I'm worried about the garden, too."

Shouting, full of fun, Wyd, Jeff, and freckle-faced little Andy ran panting up the stairs to catch a young bearded youth who seemed to have leapt straight up from the cabin deck. He was twentyish, shaggy, and barefoot. He waved cheerfully as he jumped by, then, swinging on to some bars, reached the top deck, laughing loudly. Bubbling with happiness, the three children ran after him, taking the safer stairway. Jeff and Wyd were thrilled to have playmates.

I disengaged myself as gently as I could and found Alex still talking with the Taylors.

"Andy's seven," Sallie smiled cheerfully at me. "How old are yours?"

"Seven and eight. Who's the other fellow?"

"That's Bob, with the beard. He's a dear. Robin and I first met him on Karachi Beach about ten days ago. We weren't allowed on board until last night and couldn't afford a hotel. I can't tell you how dirty and cold it was. Bob made it all seem bearable."

It was the constancy with which the ship vibrated its ill will that disturbed me. From what cold core did it emanate?

Bob approached, barefoot and smiling, a child tugging either hand.

"Hi!" He greeted us with seemingly unquenchable good spirits.

We introduced ourselves and welcomed him aboard We stood around talking until it was time for lunch. As we were about to descend the wooden stairs I whispered in Alex's ear:

"Are our passports safe?"

"Yes, I have them with me. Why?"

I pointed with my eyes. "That sailor is growing a beard."

He glanced over in surprise.

"What's the matter?" Robin asked, alerted.

Alex moved so that his back was against the railing. "That sailor has a beard. I know it sounds crazy, but Balkans never grow beards until they're old. It's a sign of losing your virility."

"Maybe he lost his virility," Robin replied uncertainly.

"It's hard to be sure," I said. "We've had to give up trying to outguess them. Alex's passport has a man with a beard, and you know already the nonsense the captain pulls about passports."

"What would they use your passport for?" Sally asked.

Bob snorted. "You guys are nuts. Anyone can get their own passports in this day and age. Why would they want yours?"

"Not everyone can get western passports," Alex corrected. "And there's always someone in the world who could use one, even just for a night in Bombay. But if you're going to use mine – or yours – you'll need a beard. You should know that if you're traveling."

Bob took the warning with a cheerful scoff. "Yeah, sure."

"Robin was telling us that the captain wouldn't let them off the ship last night."

"He probably had his reasons. He's the captain."

I was indignant at Bob's contempt for our unease. Like cats with a bird, I knew we toyed with the flutterings of something real. Still, I remembered that until I had seen explosives actually being unloaded in Bombay even I half-thought we had invented threats without roots in reality.

We're merely children playing house, I though, irritation filling me like a sponge. Reason gets suspended like a hat on a hook whenever anyone wants to think it's all make-believe.

18. OFF TO MALABAR

Skipping Along the Coast

The Jessenice carved its way around India and the ocean had once again enveloped us in warmth. We were glad to put the icy winds of Karachi far behind. Sudden hot breezes flapped at us like festive flags as we sailed south along the Malabar Coast.

The children searched for Malabar on the globe. Finding it toward the bottom, they swirled it until southern India lay on top. They braced it with a pile of books. Among the books was Robert Louis Stevenson's modest masterpiece: "A Child's Garden of Verses."

> *Where shall we adventure today that we're afloat?*
> *Wary of the weather, and steering by a star.*
> *Shall it be to Africa, a-steering of the boat?*
> *To Providence, or Babylon, or off to Malabar?*

137

We had sailed due south for almost a week, and were not to stop again until we reached Madras on the other side of India. We would circle the continent's southernmost promontory over Christmas, proceed northeast through the Straits of Ceylon, then steam north along the east coast of India to Madras. Black soot from the diesel engines rained down on the top decks, making them unlivable. We surmised the fuel was like the Bombay water: cheap and dirty. Our ship had become a tangled mess of rusty, dusty metal on the back cargo deck and rotting Spanish onions up front that were beginning to smell as we neared the equator.

"What are we going to do about Christmas?" I'd spoken through the open porthole to Alex, who was lying on a deck chair in the shade just outside our cabin, thumbing through a pile of books. He groaned.

"We have to do something for the children," I said. "They expect it. You know they still believe in Santa Claus."

Grace drifted along the passenger deck. "Christmas is hell," she remarked sweetly. She had a stack of Christmas cards from Karachi to show us, which was why it had swum into her mind at the same time it had surfaced in ours. "I've been aboard ship three times for Christmas and I can assure you it is pure hell."

Well, that sets the tone all right, I thought. We examined her lace and tinsel encrusted cards. "I'm so tired of the whole thing," she continued, smiling.

"We're going to give it a try," I said. Pulling my head back from the porthole, I went in search of the children. Maybe they would have some ideas.

Later, when Alex joined us in their cabin, Wyd held up a list:

"The people who will come to our party," she beamed, reading aloud, "are Daddy and Mummy, Stefan, Bob, Andy, Andy's Mummy and Daddy, Harold, Bertha, Arabella, two Anderssons, and two Rikstoffers."

"Sounds great," Alex said. "How many is that?"

"Fourteen," Jeff said, immediately.

"Guests," Wyd added. "We're not counting us."

First, we painted colorful invitations. Then began the long process of providing presents for everyone. Each would receive a two-foot high cone of heavy hand-painted paper decorated with tinsel, crammed with handmade gifts. There were to be little clay figures, paintings, finger-woven belts made of straw for the men, long gorgeous, Karachi glass necklaces for the women, small painted flags appropriate to each person, and a portrait of each, all done by the children, Andy Taylor included. Each gift was wrapped in paper hand-painted for the occasion. The days passed cheerfully, in cutting, pasting, sewing, drawing, reading and writing, plus games in the lounge with Bertha or Arabella, a 'skipping' tag on deck with Bob or Bjorn, and once again, sounding the gong around corridors and decks for mealtime.

I hoped that the gifts created by the children would become their own invisible Santa Claus coats. Those in turn, perhaps would be strong enough to last a lifetime, for they were woven from the threads of many happy, work-filled days.

Christmas did not loom so grimly after all.

19. INDIAN OCEAN

Mirrors

The day before Christmas there were twelve cones spread across the children's bureau, shining up into the mirror, hand-decorated and filled with presents. Invitations had been hand-delivered. The cabin was back in order. Alex and I relished the display.

Arabella knocked and came in.

"Grace says she's not religious," she told us, eyeing the gifts. "She's not going to join your party."

She walked over to the bureau and looked at herself in the mirror. She was wearing brown shorts and a long sleeved brown cotton shirt, the bright red of her lipstick her only color. Looking, she got no response from the person in the mirror.

"And the Rikstoffers say they don't approve of the sentimentality Americans have for Santa Claus. 'Christmas is real,' they say."

Bjorn pranced up to the open door, protruding pneumatically from his pink bikini. He stopped on the threshold, then, crossing both arms high on his hairy chest, he stood on tiptoe, glistening with oil and sweat. "Alex – Jane – I promise I will not renege! I am civilized! I am a man of the world. I know about honoring one's word. I am not like Harold."

"Harold?"

Bjorn uncrossed his arms and slowly came down off tiptoes. He lifted one leg slightly and revolved a sandaled foot. "Oui. Harold. He has gone to his cabin. He says he will not come out until Christmas is over."

"We all know Bertha's a little sick," Arabella said, turning her back on the mirror.

Bjorn put his foot down and grinned: "I just happened to pass their door. Stefan was taking them their breakfast. I stopped to be polite. Harold does not know about courtesy. After all, he is only a *petit operateur*. He said he would not appear until Christmas is over. He said 'to hell with the whole bloody lot!' Both he and Bertha are fine, I say."

"I think you're being awfully hard on poor Harold," said Arabella.

"See?" he hissed meaningfully. Pivoting, he pranced down the corridor.

Arabella headed towards the door. "Harold is very upset because you didn't ask him to be Santa Claus."

"You're kidding!"

"Bertha is upset also. She feels you didn't consult her."

"Heavens, what about?"

"Plans. We think you should have formed a committee."

"A committee!" Alex exploded in laughter and slipped away hurriedly.

"I wouldn't know how to form a committee." I said to Arabella. "Why don't you or Bertha form a committee, for heaven's sake!"

"Oh, my! I didn't mean to get you upset."

Bjorn's face re-appeared in the open porthole: "Would you have joined their committee, Jane?" He laughed. "Remember," he added gleefully. "Christmas is hell!"

141

Arabella caught one last sight of herself in the mirror, and left.

"My friend, you and I are very much alike. We are excitable, but we are civilized. No matter what happens, you can count on me." He popped from view.

I took a deep breath. These were exasperating incantations. The more so in that he was probably right. First, Christmas was obviously going to be more difficult than anticipated. Second, that no amount of good intentions on my part could alter the fact that I was as least as irritating to the others as Bjorn was to me.

At least Bjorn had an excuse. He was walking around with death in his skull. He was close to a grand flare of a death, which would burn everything up at once. For me, death came in small doses, little deaths to die as I went along: deaths of the heart, of friendships, of good will, of trust, and all that.

Maybe all the passengers were reflections of my own mixed-up self, in a funhouse of mirrors. Just the thought of Arabella made me bristle, yet somehow she personified my own self-righteousness and unexamined bluster. Then there was Harold whose his armless rigidities challenged me painfully. I missed his potential kindness, suffering the mean truth that I was armless myself – unable to reach to him.

Who knows, I mused, looking out the empty porthole, if all our friends were not simply undeveloped extensions of ourselves, mirror images of those unarticulated selves we hoped to ignore by inaction? Travel activated the undeveloped sides in us, the Greek, the Egyptian, or Indian: perhaps people did too. Perhaps only a hermit could pull all the friends he needed out of his own self.

We are made to be integrated personalities. Somebody just spilled us around the countryside: we exist more vividly in the concrete realities of an acquaintance than in the amorphous churning of what we think is our self.

As for our new passengers, the Wests' cheerfully unconcealed contempt for our vague doubts and suspicions easily matched my own scorn for their egotistical naiveté. But even they were already succumbing to the ill-will that imbued our soot-sprinkled white ship.

Bob, too. I envied Bob his gravity-defying ability to jump from deck to deck, ignoring the reproaches of crew and passengers as he ran by, trailing three little cheered-up children like the tail of a kite. But lately he, too, tended to disappear into his cabin. Bob's good nature was not nearly enough to melt the fierce cold of this tiny fragment of humanity. Was there any one in the world, who could? Stefan came to mind. He offered the mystery of kindness, tentatively, modestly tendered. For me to claim so much would be "proud and vain," as the kids would say. If anything, Stefan reflected my ghostlike aspect, as I moved restlessly around the world, and about the boat – uncommitted but still not free.

It was a curious clutch of spiritual doppelgangers that gave me no comfort. As usual for that, I could, and always did, turn to Alex and the children.

* * *

The afternoon of Christmas Eve passed silent and hot. The mood of the ship was sullen. The captain had forbidden any of the crew to appear above decks, either during the afternoon or evening, except on specified duty.

The Taylors retired in disgust to their cabin. The Clements locked their doors. By this point even Bob was contemptuous of our fatheaded efforts at festivity. I was bothered by Bob's attitude in particular. The young and good-natured do not know how easy it is to twist their very goodness into obstruction. They have been told they are innocent and that somehow innocence is like goodness. But innocence is amoral. It can turn in any direction when it is disturbed.

Our final task before the party was to decorate the Christmas tree, which we'd bought in Karachi. It was about two feet high, made of translucent, moss green paper. Its exquisitely cut branches floated gracefully to the gentle rolling of the ship. The children had made inch-high, paper candy canes, and silver baskets just big enough for one small chocolate. They had cut silver and gold stars, and small spirals. Each was carefully hung on the tree by silver threads. Also an inch-wide circle, one triangle, one little square, one pentagon, and atop the tree a silver star. Everything was tiny and very light. Five tiny silver Christmas bulbs found a place. The last to go on were three half-sized candy lifesavers that added transparent sweetness to the overall luster.

Alex, Jeff, Wyd, little Andy Taylor, and I formed a circle around the completed tree. Its odd magic lit up each face, and seemed to spread a tender glow throughout the lounge. Where had this tiny miracle come from?

Stefan entered: "Missus, I am sorry."

"What's the matter now?" Alex asked.

"Captain forbid festivities in the public lounge."

"Your captain better try telling me that face to face," Alex said.

Stefan straightened nervously. "He is captain. This be his kingdom. Also it be against the Communist State to allow public worship of the Christ."

"My friend, he may not like dirty warmongering capitalists like Jeff and Wyd," Alex was firm. "But no one's going to cheer him in the streets when he gets home if he makes trouble over a children's party."

"Stefan, it's most unlikely Christ will be present at this party," I added.

"Go tell the captain to jump off his bridge or at least come and talk to us directly," Alex said.

Unsmiling, Stefan left, but his eyes were twinkling.

I spread out decorations for walls and tables. A photo of Tito, the firm-faced Yugoslav dictator, dominated the festive scene. I caught sight of Alex staring at it, and grabbed his arm: "You can't decorate him. They'll throw us overboard."

Wyd came dejectedly into our cabin while Alex and I were getting dressed.

"What's the matter?" I asked.

She struggled with tears. I picked her up and cuddled her for a while.

"Tell me what happened," I whispered. The last thing we needed tonight was a fight between the children. "Maybe it was a misunderstanding."

Wyd gulped. "Andy said there's no Santa. He said that – that he found out because he stayed up one Christmas and he saw his Mummy put out all his presents under the tree."

"Oh."

"He's lying, isn't he, Mummy?" Wyd asked anxiously.

Luckily, I'd been preparing for this inevitable moment.

"Wyd," I said. "Tonight will be an important night for everyone. For you, too. You're going to find out for yourself who Santa is. Most people never know."

Wyd looked relieved. "Will Jeff and Andy find out too?"

I nodded. "They don't know it yet," I said conspiratorially, "Yes, there really is a Santa, but he's a very secret Santa with a secret name. Tonight you're going to learn his secret name."

Reassured, Wyd hopped off my lap. "I'll go tell them." She skipped happily out of the cabin.

"What on earth are you going to do?" Alex asked.

"Put the kids through an initiation, sort of."

"How?"

"By telling them a story. If I'm successful, it will last the rest of their lives."

"What if it doesn't work?"

"No harm done," I replied. "Just the usual thickening of the soul."

"Okay!" Alex said, gaining enthusiasm. "Let's go to their cabin."

The children had made themselves Merlin-style hats: tall, painted-paper cones covered with hieroglyphs of tinsel and sparkles, topped by a fountain of streamers. They had cut pieces of white paper into long thin strips, pasting enough together to make their beards. Their Madras cotton shirts and red corduroy pants with red rubber boots served splendidly as Santa costumes. The wide mirror caught their intensity. Even Andy, who had entered into the preparations skeptically, now sailed a sea of dreams as vast as the one outside.

"Do you know who Santa Claus is?" I asked them.

"My Mummy," said Andy, immediately.

"I mean the real, real Santa Claus.

"You don't mean Jesus?" Andy's freckled face was set against such easy allegory.

"No, that's not what I mean. We have time before the party to tell the real story, so let's all sit quietly to listen."

Alex settled with the children on one bunk. I sat across on the other.

I had made up the story so I was a little nervous telling it for the first time.

20. "SANTA CLAUS'S SECRET NAME"

I Tell a Story

*O*nce upon a time there lived a Little Girl and a Little Boy. They were called the Curious Children. One frosty day they went to the Old Woman and asked her to tell them about Santa Claus. They knew the story well, but they loved to hear it told again and again.

'My little friends,' the Old Woman said, 'the time has come for you to find Santa Claus.'

'Why?' asked the Little Boy.

'To learn his Secret Name or forget him forever,' the Old Woman said.

'How can we find him?' asked the Little Girl.

The Old Woman answered: 'When night falls and the stars come out, light a candle. By its light write a letter asking Santa to visit you. Then read it out loud. Santa will hear the words as they turn to light, and he will come.'

The Curious Children thanked her and went off to do what they were told. When it was dark, they lit a candle. They wrote their letter and then, by the light of the candle's flame, they read it out loud. Suddenly they heard a friendly laugh. They looked up to see sparkling before them the great and marvelous figure of Santa Claus. He was dressed all in red with snow-white trimming. A belt of radiant coals glowed around his ample middle. His hair and beard curled fire.

'What do you want?' he asked in a kindly tone.

'We came to ask you your Secret Name,' the Little Girl whispered.

'The Old Woman sent us,' the Little Boy explained.

Santa nodded his great head. 'You are brave and curious children. It is time. Come with me.'

Lifting them up onto his sleigh, he flew into the night. Over darkened treetops and the lights of the towns that sparkled far below, they flew together. Santa took them into an open field in the very center of which they saw a blazing bonfire. Moss-covered rocks big enough to sit on encircled the flames. Around them the Curious Children saw small figures dancing. They looked like the great and marvelous Santa himself.

Everyone settled quietly onto the soft, green rocks.

Santa spoke: 'For seven long years you have worked for me as you promised. You have worked well. Tonight you fulfill the rest of your promise. You must answer my question or forget me forever.'

A hush fell over the listeners.

'Tell me,' Santa said. 'What is my Secret Name?'

A hush fell over our little cabin, too. I looked around at my listeners.

"Close your eyes," I whispered.

They closed their eyes as I went on.

The Curious Children closed their eyes while they guessed. In the dark they could see a brightness like a galaxy spiraling inwards.

'That's right,' they heard Santa say. 'You are close to the Secret Name.'

The children moved towards the fire. Could anyone find the answer? Would it not be lovely to find the answer? They would tell others, and help them never to forget Santa Claus. Over the Curious Children there crept a warm feeling of friendliness. They began to feel very cheerful. They felt like the little Santas sitting with them. The Little Boy jumped up and turned a somersault. The Little Girl jumped up and stretched out like a star.

'I know the Name,' shouted the Little Girl.

"I know the Secret Name,' shouted the Little Boy.

'Go ahead,' laughed Santa. 'Help others guess the Secret Name.'

I paused. The children's eyes were still closed, waiting. Alex's flickered open. One by one the children opened their eyes as well.

"Can you guess the secret name?" I asked.

"I know it's my Mummy," Andy insisted.

I looked at Alex.

"St. Nicholas?" he suggested.

"No. That's one of the names people call him. Remember, only Santa can say his secret name and mean himself when he says it."

Jeff frowned.

"Family?" Wyd said slowly. "Someone in your family, like a brother?"

I shook my head.

"A pet?" Andy said, feeling braver. "I got a puppy once for Christmas."

"Not it."

"The moon."

"The stars."

"No."

"Love?" Alex suggested.

I shook my head.

"Giving?"

149

"Nothing like that. It's a real person. That's what you have to remember."

"Kris Kringle?"

"An elf?"

"King Wenceslas?"

"Think of it this way. What does Santa do?"

"He's supposed to give presents," Andy said, looking discouraged. "But we know he doesn't because he doesn't exist."

Wyd looked at him with disapproval.

"Who does give presents then?" I asked.

"My mother."

"Who else?"

"Daddy?"

"Who else?"

He tried to think.

"Wyd, you tell me something about Santa."

"He's friendly," she said.

"And very jolly and he says 'ho ho ho'!" Jeff added.

"Okay, now who else is friendly and jolly and says 'ho ho ho'? Who else gives presents? Santa means only himself when he says his Secret Name."

"I don't get it." Jeff was very puzzled.

"I mean, if you want him to come to you, I can't call him, or anyone else. Each of you does that for yourself. That's why you have to find the Secret Name for yourselves. Find the Secret Name and say it out loud, and you can only mean the real Santa Claus."

"Oh," said Alex suddenly. "Oh." He began laughing.

"Daddy's found it," Wyd smiled.

"I think I have." He stood up and took a few steps, chuckling.

"It's impossible!" cried Andy.

"It can't be impossible if Daddy guessed it," Jeff pointed out reasonably, encouraged by Alex's success.

"Let me see. Santa's Secret Name..." Alex murmured.

Jeff was deep in thought. "Only I can say it – " He looked up, understanding dawning. "Oh."

"Is it me?" asked Wyd.

```"Me?"``` Andy looked at her in surprise.

"Just a sec," I said. "Santa wouldn't say 'I am me'. What would Santa say?"

"I is Santa?" Wyd asked, still a bit shaky on her grammar.

"I am Santa Claus," Jeff said firmly.

Andy took a deep breath, then slowly as if to himself: "I am? Is? Santa Claus?"

Alex sat back down, relishing the radiant faces.

"Let me go on with the story," I said.

'I am Santa!' cried the Little Girl.
'I am Santa!' cried the Little Boy.
Everyone jumped up together, chorusing: 'I am Santa Claus!'
Jolly old Santa Claus laughed and laughed. 'You have guessed my Secret Name. If you ever need me, say it. We can work together always.'

There was silence as the story sank in. Then the children stood up, and for a long minute the three little Santas looked in the mirror. Then they put on their hats, adjusted their beards, wiggled their toes into their rubber boots. Slowly they picked up their presents, straightened their backs, and walked to the lounge for final preparations.

They were chanting in time to the waves: "And I myself am Santa Claus."
```

21. CHRISTMAS EVE

Silent Night

At seven on the dot, Bjorn materialized in the middle of the lounge. "I won't desert you!" he laughed. He was immaculately dressed in a light blue suit, grey handkerchief impeccably folded in his breast pocket, matching silk socks and tie.

"*Oui*! I know people say Christmas is hell," he went on expansively, "but it is for the children. My two children, they choose to stay with the money." (I later argued Bjorn had said 'Mummy,' but Alex insisted it was 'money.') "They don't choose me."

"Too bad," I said.

"Well, they can't be in two places at once," Alex said helpfully.

"*Non*. It breaks my heart. But they are horrible children. Only at Christmas I care. I tell Grace how brave you are and that we must stand by you tonight. She is getting dressed now. I carry my gold cigarette case. Look!"

He pulled it out to show us, along with golden cigar-clippers on a gold chain. Replacing them, he stretched out his hand so we could admire his diamond rings.

"Ah, but you look perfect," he turned his flattering attention to me.

I wore a blue and silver gown bought at an Indian bazaar. Gaudy Pakistani slippers encased my feet, and silver earrings dangled like tiny frozen fountains from my ears. My hair was still free and long.

"Only you could look beautiful in such a costume," he amended. Turning to the children, he started yodeling: "Jangle Bells, Jangle Bells, jangle all the way!"

Alex joined in, laughing, and the children soon followed. The cones were laid out across the couch. As guests arrived, they were given one by the bubbling children. Arabella came first wearing a crimson hair band in her hennaed hair, a low-cut red evening gown, and red satin slippers. The Taylors came in their usual T-shirts & shorts, more cheerful than I'd expected. Then the three little Santa Clauses aggressively forced their good cheer on those entrenched in their cabins. When Bob saw the children's efforts he bounded out like a large puppy dog and danced down the corridor with them, shouting gay Christmas nonsense.

He pounded on Harold's cabin door.

Harold opened it, glaring. It took him a moment to sort things out. Chagrined to discover it was not Alex but the three children who had usurped his coveted role as Santa Claus, he sheepishly took the two cones they offered and said he and Bertha would ready themselves for the party.

Bob laughed: "Let's go see if the Germans want to change their minds as well."

The children returned happily to announce that the Germans were coming.

Grace sat on the couch at the far end of the room, vague and resplendent in a long, white evening gown, which clung tightly to her

153

well-corseted figure. Arabella talked loudly to her, holding a long, slim tortoise shell cigarette holder with an equally slim Egyptian unlit cigarette. Bjorn went over to the Australians to show them his gold cigarette case. The goldsmith in Harold could not resist appraising.

Bjorn laughed at him. "It's solid," he assured him.

Harold stiffened and turned his back.

Bob proudly ushered the Rikstoffers into the party. The children asked them to come to the couch and offered them their special cones. Silently, the two old people nodded wistfully, and accepted them without a word.

"What a beautiful tree you all made," Arabella said admiringly. "I never got my pupils to make anything so delicate at their age. It's a miracle."

A little later I noticed the Rikstoffers had disappeared.

I went over to the children and asked if everything was all right.

"They took the presents into the dining room," Jeff said.

"They didn't even say thank you," Andy said. "Mom always says to say thank you."

A little desperately, I met Alex's eyes across the room. He immediately got to his feet and called for silence.

"When I roar, I want all of you to roar back," he said. "And when I stamp, all of you stamp."

Without waiting, he launched into Vachel Lindsay's poem, *The Daniel Jazz:*

> *Darius the Mede was a king and a wonder.*
> *His eyes flashed fire and his voice was thunder.*
> *He kept bad lions in a monstrous den,*
> *And fed up the lions on Christian men.*
>
> *Daniel was the butler, swagger and swell,*
> *He ran upstairs, he answered the bell.*
> *And he would let in whoever came a'calling:*
> *Saints so holy, scamps so appalling!*

With a loud crash, the lounge door was flung open.

"Silence!" the first mate shouted, his voice high-pitched with anger. "Captain orders you be silent! You are disrupting the spirit of the ship by this noise! Celebration of the Christ is forbidden by our state!"

While the words were being spat into the silence, Bjorn crept around the side of the room towards the door. Calmly he shut it in the man's furious face and locked the door. Alex picked up the rhythm and finished the poem with a lot of roaring and stamping from us all; perhaps even a bit more than before.

When that was over everyone clapped loudly, feeling more relaxed. Stefan unlocked the door and escorted the wretched first mate over to the bar, pouring him a slivovic without speaking. Harold also fetched drinks from the little bar, and offered his familiar toast: "May the bottom be a mile down."

As usual in mid-ocean, it produced a disconcerting moment of insecurity.

"I do think the captain is crazy to be so disapproving of everything we do," Sally Taylor said to me. "Christmas is Christmas, after all."

Arabella joined us: "It was very naughty of you not to tell us the children were going to play Santa Claus. If we'd known that, none of us would have been upset. Don't you think Harold looks gorgeous in tweeds? But Bertha looks like she should be in bed, if you ask me."

Sweat darkened Bertha's pink organdy blouse and she rocked unsteadily, a drink in her hand as usual.

I stepped into the dining-room, wanting to be alone.

"Jangle bells, jangle bells." Voices floated from the lounge: Bjorn was unquashable.

The party had its own momentum now, no longer my affair. The tension was inside me.

I looked around vaguely. There on the Rikstoffers' dining table were two cones. Why do people like to be dreary, I wondered. Why couldn't they have been more receptive to the children? Why couldn't they be happy? How did they think the children would feel when they saw them there, unopened, unwanted? What on earth was in their tiny, selfish minds? All the anger at the lack of fun leading up to the party surfaced in me. I grabbed the two cones, pulled open the door

155

into the corridor, then pushed open the heavy door onto the steamy, hot deck. A few dim deck lights pierced a tunnel through blackness. The ship's whiteness was greyed by night.

Furious, I threw the cones overboard into the foaming black water.

I was surprised but grateful when the three children joined me on deck, shepherded by Stefan. "I think they need fresh air," he explained, peering down at the black water.

I couldn't see his expression. The kids relished the fresh air and began running up and down.

Leaning over the railing, watching the black waves rush away from the ship's side, I felt reassured by Stefan's presence. Otherwise there was no stirring of sailor activity anywhere. Soon I knew something was wrong: the feeling was as palpable as the wet dark. The strands of relationships on board ship lay coiled like snakes in a basket. A fall, a drunken brawl, could turn sinister tonight.

I shouldn't be out here now.

"I'd better go back," I said suddenly. "Shall I take the kids?"

"No! No. Let them stay with me." There was warning in his voice. I looked up sharply. The children, still wearing their beards and hats, were skipping up and down the deck.

"The air is good for them," Stefan added hastily.

Without a word I left them. They were safe with him. I could count on that. Hurrying back to the lounge, I entered into glacial silence. Captain Stanislav stood with his back to the bar, facing the room. A sailor hovered behind him like a giant shadow cast on the wall. Alex stood facing him from across the room, his back to the prow.

"You!" The virulence of the captain's tone was like a shot. He pointed at Alex. "Come here!"

Alex remained where he was, unmoving. The rest of the passengers, too, remained completely motionless as though they were playing a game of statues. Even Bjorn, caught balancing on one foot, a glass in his hand, made no movement, although he winked at me as he kept his balance.

The captain strode over to Alex. "I am captain of this ship. You do as you are told. Do you understand?"

Alex's brawny, bearded form went eye to eye with him; yet the sailor on the captain's heels made even Alex look small.

My heart jumped. I could hardly breathe.

Alex slowly cupped one fist in the other, pondering. I closed my eyes. *You can't hit the captain,* I tried to send my thoughts across the room. *He's the captain, Alex. You can't hit the captain. It's the law of the oceans.*

"From now on you will do as I tell you," Captain Stanislav commanded furiously. "Do you understand?"

Alex's eyes flashed dark. I could almost hear him counting to ten.

"No," he said at last.

The sailor took a step. There was a rustle from passengers.

"You have been disrupting the spirit of my ship."

Alex shoved his hands into his pockets and took a step backwards: "I have?"

"What spirit is that?" I was feeling braver now Alex's hands were in his pockets.

"Hush!" Alex ordered tightly, without looking back.

The captain ignored me. He took another menacing step towards Alex: "When I order you do not have party, you do not."

Alex remained silent.

"When I say you do not leave my ship, you do not leave it. I am captain!"

Alex's eyes narrowed again. "We have the proper visas. Since you plan to be docked for a certain number of days, there is no reason we know of why we should be kept aboard. Is there one we don't know of?"

"Yes!" Captain Stanislav announced. "You are nothing but cheap smugglers!"

You could see the words settling through Alex like gold flakes floating down through clear water. His elbows lifted his hands visibly, then it was a struggle between his hands and elbows, finally his fists settled once more deep into his pants pockets. His face was without expression. I edged closer to him. If he tried to hit out, I would intervene. Under no circumstances could he strike the captain. It is the first commandment.

Alex spoke softly: "Now, Captain, you know that's not true."

"You are a trouble maker, a law-breaker."

"I'll try my best to conform to the spirit of your ship from now on," Alex said.

"You take orders from me from now on." The captain's tone froze the air between them. "I am the law! You Americans think you own the world. You are all troublemakers! It must stop, understand? It must stop immediately!"

"You've made yourself clear."

For twenty seconds their eyes locked together. Then the captain turned and stalked out of the room. The giant sailor followed on his heels, his face impassive.

The passengers broke out into nervous chatter all at once.

"You were wonderful!" Arabella gushed.

"I say, you put the old boy right in his place," Harold nodded. "He has no right to behave so abominably to his passengers. No British captain would."

Bjorn approached Alex and shook his hand: "I tell my wife, you may look like a stupid American in those shorts, but you are a genius! You have a deep soul; I am the only one here who understands you. I borrowed your books from the captain. He wants to know what's in them. I tell him nothing political."

"I think you were splendid," Grace said, standing up and smoothing the folds of her dress. "Quite terrifying, in fact."

"It's all right now," Alex said, looking at me.

"Where are the children?" asked Sally, suddenly worried.

"They're on deck," I said. "Stefan's with them."

"I'll go get them," Robin said. "I could do with a drink. Alex could too. I'll tell Stefan."

"Honey, what do you think he wanted?" Arabella said, still looking shaky.

"The bastard wanted me to hit him," Alex answered curtly.

"But why you?" I asked.

"Maybe he thinks I really was smuggling."

"Well, you did disappear for a week in India without informing anyone," Arabella remarked. "He knows you didn't go to your embassy, which is strange."

Bjorn grinned: "You controlled yourself admirably. I would have slapped the disgusting man, he would have slapped me, and all would be over for me."

Robin returned with Stefan trailing the three children. Their cheeks were pink with excitement and cold. The very lateness of the hour lent magic to their happiness.

Stefan looked blankly at me. I projected a silent thanks.

"Jangle bells! Jangle bells!" came from the middle of the room as Bjorn broke into Christmas song. Holding hands, three laughing children joined him to begin a circle.

Robin brought Bertha to stand beside Bjorn, as Sally encouraged Bob and the Andersons to join them. They put their arms around each other's shoulders, waving Alex and me over. Wyd went over to pull Arabella towards the group. Harold touchily refused to come in beside Bjorn, walking ostentatiously around until he was behind Bob and Robin. Pushing them apart, he stepped between them.

Alex asked Stefan to join us as the children hopped into the center, their beards crumpled, their eyes shining. I stood between Stefan and Alex, as *We Three Kings* faded into silence. After a few more carols, Alex started *Silent Night*. Harold boomed out the carol in a thick Yorkshire accent.

The Taylors joined in, bringing London sounds along with their higher pitch. Arabella poured out a twangy Florida warble.

Bjorn whispered loudly to Alex: "We stick by you to the end, Alex! You see that."

He picked up the carol in Danish. Grace joined him.

Stefan's dark eyes were wet as he gazed lovingly at the children, while softly singing *Silent Night* in his own Serbian. The first mate came in to stand silently at the door. His lips moved quietly in song too.

The children's wonder filled the room, lightening the darkness in the hearts of the grown-ups, reaching to fill the black immensity through which our little vessel floated.

My own sense of wonder was bounded with hoops of steely distrust and skepticism. When you are even a bit skeptical, does it do away with innocence as a pin does with the air in a balloon? Looking at the happy children instead of into my own heart, I knew it could not be so. The promise was too wondrous never to be fulfilled – too generous to collapse at the first pinprick – or even the last.

Our voices became lower, slower. Silent Night came to an end. We stayed entwined for a moment longer. Then we quietly said good night and went to our cabins.

23. SEVEN WHALES

The Opposite of Santa

Alex and the children had gone ahead, and I was a little late when I met Bjorn on my way to breakfast the next morning.

"Jane!" Bjorn exclaimed in real dismay. "Why did you throw the Rikstoffer's cones overboard last night? They are Christians, Jane. They open their presents at Christmas morning. You knew that. They were very happy the children made them presents. They did not expect it. No one did," he added accusingly. "Someone saw what you did. They told. I am surprised at you, Jane."

I was appalled and deeply ashamed. Of course I knew that people celebrate different holiday rituals. I try to abide by all of them.

Why had I forgotten last night?

"It was petty of you. They are very old and last night they were very tired. The children would have loved to see the old woman and the old man opening their presents one by one in the peace and quiet of this morning's breakfast. Why did you do it?"

"I know," I said forlornly. "You're right,"

"You also know they come from Dresden, Jane. You know what that means."

In a horrific flash, I remembered that, too. Numbly, I nodded.

"Yes. You Americans bombed Dresden when the war was essentially over. There was no need. You burned one of the most beautiful cities of the world. Even the Germans spared Paris, Florence, Rome. The Rikstoffers were in Dresden during the American bombing. *Oui*! Day and night. They lived in bombed out basements, but their friends did not. Their families did not. They died. Can you understand what it means for them to be on this boat, close to you Americans?"

He turned like a cat and went into the dining room by himself.

I wanted to run to my cabin. Instead, I knew I had to go into face breakfast.

The Andersons had chosen to sit with the Rikstoffers. It was a statement. Arabella joined in their conversation from her table, fingering the necklace of red Karachi glass the children had made for her. The cheery Taylors, Sally with her green bead necklace and Robin proudly wearing his handmade belt, sat nearby. The Clements were also wearing the children's presents: a belt for one, a flashing purple necklace for the other. A deeply contented Andy was sitting with a very proud Jeff and an equally happy Wyd at their own table.

People had broken barriers. Santa had come.

Giving them time to move away if that should be their wish, I slowly made my way between the tables and stood beside the ancient couple.

"I am sorry about last night, I did not think. I thought you didn't care," I said and bowed to them.

Without hesitation, the Rikstoffers looked up and bowed back in quiet Christmas forgiveness. A larger forgiveness.

"We had Christmas at sea," Jeff reported in his book as we rounded the southern tip of India. "I was Santa Claus and made all my own presents to give to everyone. We saw seven whales blowing by on Christmas morning."

Thin morning mists evaporated into a gentle blue sky. A hint of the vast Pacific, not too much further east, pulsed through a welcome cool turbulence. The seven whales were close to the freighter. Dark grey and enormous, they swam past in train, shooting rainbow spume into the dawn. The children had never seen a whale before. Alex and I had, but not seven of them together, and not on Christmas morning.

For some precious moments I had been the opposite of Santa. I would remember that for the rest of my life.

As we counted the seven whales, I wished even then that I had been free enough, been able enough, to give the little German woman and the tiny German man each a hug.

23. ON THE COAST OF COROMANDEL

Dravidian Copra Loaders

The waves beneath the ship curled into increasingly original patterns. Cold Antarctic currents collided with warm ones from the north. The ship had been heavily loaded in Bombay, but even so the blue tetrahedrons of water now pushed us higher and lower than before. The freighter stitched its way northward along the Coast of Coromandel.

Jeff and Wyd sat backwards on their deckchairs, in the shade outside our cabin, using them as tables. I was helping them to write and draw figures in their books. Stefan passed us, and then returned, smiling, to listen as Jeff read his work out loud. He seemed in no hurry to move on. But the children eventually rushed away to find Bob.

"How long have you been on Jessenice?" I asked Stefan.

"Since the war."

Twenty years! "What did you do before the war?"

"I was a young man. I went to university. I study philosophy."

"I suppose traveling on a freighter is also a form of philosophy."

Stefan smiled. "This is true. Since going to sea, I be better philosopher."

"Are the trips you take always the same?"

"Depends on cargo."

"What do we do at Coromandel?"

"We load copra there, but there is no going ashore. There is no port. It just be jungle."

"What's copra?"

"Coconut kernel. They make coconut oil from copra."

"Stefan, have you tried to get a job on another boat? Wouldn't you rather work for someone else? On a passenger ship, maybe?"

"I cannot."

"Why?"

"It is complicated. I am indebted to Captain."

"Indebted? How?"

Stefan hesitated. "We used to be like – brothers. He saved my life in the war. Now he needs me."

"It's been a long time, now. Aren't you even?"

"A life is all anyone possess. Every day I am grateful for mine."

I wondered what had happened. Had they, like so many families during a revolution, been torn apart by warring ideologies? Had Stefan, in his quiet way, worked with the Resistance, and been caught? Had the captain, on the winning side, stepped in to save him?

It added a dimension to captain, imagining him and Stefan 'like brothers.'

Next day we anchored within sight of the steaming sub-continent. Our ship rocked gently, as if to itself, between a very low sandbar and, in the distance, an unbroken green jungle wall. A jungle, hot, mysterious and, for the purposes of the freighter, rich in copra. It offered no harbor, no town.

To the evident anxiety of the officers, we would be loading copra for about three days, anchored several miles out to sea. We were directly in the path of the monsoons so that, should we get a warning of impending storms, we would have to speed immediately for open waters. The captain, in the meantime, eased the ship behind a sand bar that he chose to use as a slight break to the ocean swells which badgered us. It was a dangerous move to make, but it would serve to speed the copra loading.

The sea was calm on the surface but we could feel the ship roll steeply. Without the forward motion the effect was exaggerated. The unfamiliar motion made us all queasy.

In the relative cool of evening a small fleet of Dravidian sampans and small copra-heavy rafts appeared over the tops of the long, smooth swells. Rope ladders were lowered, the ship's cranes swung into action, and work began. The swells increased, and the ship lurched back and forth.

I sat on Wyd's bed, telling children stories after dinner. Our cozy cabin helped dispel our queasiness. Together we twisted the sickening roll to our own purposes, loudly chanting a poem by Edward Lear to the rhythm of the ocean swells:

> *On the Coast of Coromandel*
> *Where the early pumpkins blow*
> *In the middle of the woods,*
> *Lives the Yonghy Bonghy Bo.*
> *One small chair without a candle,*
> *One small jug without a handle,*
> *These were all the worldly goods*
> *In the middle of the woods,*
> *These were all the worldly goods,*
> *Of the Yonghy Bonghy Bo*
> *Of the Yonghy Bonghy Bo.*

Chanting the poem made the lurching less severe. Then I realized that we were not reciting the poem to the rhythm of the sea any longer. The ship was not moving at all. I did not share the children's relief. When the poem ended, I kissed them goodnight and went to investigate.

On deck the heat was intense. The air was marbled with unfamiliar odors, undissolved by the least stirrings in the atmosphere.

I found Bjorn leaning over the forward railing, his eyes intent on the precarious on-loading at sea. Two strong searchlights beamed down on the two open holds, their powerful light by-passing the rest of the deck which was lit by three softer cones of light, two near the prow, and one just under our deck near the side railing. Against the theatrical backdrop, small, graceful black figures appeared and disappeared like shadow puppets.

These were the Dravidian loaders. Being very short and slight of build, four men did the work that one beefy Balkan could have handled alone. They were lovely to watch. Their exquisite bodies, slender and small, were kept gracefully erect, and were etched clear in the backlight. Their limbs took on an independent angularity and their gestures had the surprise emphasis of shadow puppets.

Long, curly hair sprang from their heads like black sun rays. Instead of folding into fists, their tiny hands tended to splay outward as they leapt about their work. They were like black dandelions worshipping a midnight sun.

"Hi, Bjorn. What's going on?"

Bjorn came up to me, looking grave. "Do you know what the captain has done now?"

"I wondered."

"He has run us aground. It is to aid the workers."

I eyed the swirling black water. Harold approached, keeping me between himself and Bjorn.

"Bjorn says the reason we're not rolling about any longer is because we're stuck on the sandbar," I told him.

"Bjorn is a bloody liar, and you know it. If we'd run aground we'd have folded like an accordion. Just look at those swells."

"Tell him," Bjorn whispered loudly, "that it isn't the swells that ran aground."

Harold stomped off. I looked at the swells, then back to the loading deck. Copra lay scattered about in large bales. It now had to

167

be pushed into the hold by hand and stacked below. While this was being done, cranes were lifting more bales onto the deck from a line of small barges. It was all done at night because of the heat, but even so the process was hot and slow. I watched the elegant Dravidians tug and shove their outsized packages. They scrambled up and down the bales, appearing and disappearing behind the mounds they were building, laughing and talking continuously as they worked.

Beyond the group working around the hold, there were others busy at the ship's stern. They had been allowed to build a fire there to cook the day's ration of rice. Plates made of lotus leaves sewn together with palm fiber had been brought from shore. The cook piled each floppy dish with a mound of rice, then placed them on the deck around the fire. There were no implements.

With the ease of dancers, the men squatted at their meal. Orange flames glinted off their black marble bodies. They talked all the while. The strangeness of their surroundings kept them alert. Glancing over their shoulders, their black eyes searched the ship with wonder. The white freighter must have materialized out of a darkness in their own imaginations and would just as strangely soon disappear like a magician's illusion.

As a traveler, the reverse was happening to me. The relentless thrust and push of the ship made everything else ephemeral. I could no longer believe my senses. Appearances were as unreliable as intuition often is. Something always kept slipping just out of reach. I let a city into my consciousness, or a temple or a new country, and it had disappeared by morning. Things moved into focus and were gone in an instant. I felt as shadowy as the Dravidians must have thought me.

"They are crazy to allow a fire to be built," Bjorn edged closer. "The ship can go boom at any second."

"Oh, it looks pretty safe. That's a thick deck."

"Jane, you are always the same. You turn away from facts. The hold below is still filled with explosives. It is not safe at all, *non*."

"But they unloaded the explosives in Bombay. We saw them."

"*Oui*, some of it. But not all. The third mate tells me it is destined for the Vietcong." He shrugged at the Dravidians squatting around the fire. "I do not think they should be allowed."

"Have you seen Alex?" I asked.

"He is down there." Bjorn pointed grandly to the working deck below.

I leaned far over the rail in disbelief. Alex sat with Mikhail the boson on one side, and Savo the radio operator on the other. A cone of light held the three large men in its dim glow as, sweating and talking, they leaned against the onion shipment, their feet stretched out in front, their pink faces wreathed in contentment. An arc of beer bottles stood neatly beside Mikhail, a half-empty case was within reach of all three. I was astonished at their evident camaraderie. Since when had they become friends?

Mikhail's voice was addressing Alex.

"I wish to thank you for your present. Captain not allow to drink before New Year's. This be Communist feast. You know what happen? We start drinking your present early and soon is big fight below. One sailor has knife. Everyone after to kill big Mikhail. I run for cabin. Just in time. Lock door and don't come out one day and one night. Ah, it is a terrible voyage."

"A big fight," Savo jiggled with laughter. "Sailor go after big Mikhail with busted bottle." He leaned over Alex and punched the big boson on the shoulder.

A small commotion over by the makeshift kitchen caught my eye. With some relief I saw the Dravidians had finished their meal and were stomping out the fire. The stack of lotus plates was neatly put on one side for tomorrow's meal.

My attention was drawn back to Mikhail. He scratched a kitchen match with his thumbnail to light a cigarette. His sea-blue eyes followed its high, golden trajectory over the ship's side into the dark.

'Do I sail to my family, or ... the other way?"

"Do you love your wife?" Alex countered.

"I love her here!" Mikhail patted his boulder-like paunch. "I love my children, too. My three eagles." He brought out an old, bulging wallet from which he lifted battered snapshots.

"Maybe you don't sail to your family or away," Alex said, looking at the photos. "Maybe you sail right round them. They stay inside a bubble that is you."

Mikhail brooded on that for a time. "I better than a bubble," he said at last.

"Mikhail, when I see through the onionskin of your soul, I discover strange countries, continents, planets, even distant stars inside the bubble that is you."

"Why you do that?" Mikhail bent forward to listen.

"Because you're a bubble, and I'm a bubble. We're all bubbles." Alex warmed to his theme. "All bubbles, expanding in the dark of infinity."

Casually Mikhail spat over the side.

"All bubbles. All crazy," Savo explained.

Mikhail lowered his eyes and lifted both hands. I thought he was going to wrestle Alex. Casually, Alex reached for a bottle of beer, opened it and handed it to the boson. His hard-bunched face relaxed. Savo and Alex each opened their own. The three big men leaned back and sipped slowly.

"Today my birthday," Mikhail broke the silence. "Forty-five years. This mean Mikhail all through. Phaa-a! Old. In Yugoslavia, old. What happen if sailors cut Mikhail's bubble, eh?"

"You mean, what happens to the universe inside you when your bubble breaks?" Alex stopped to think about it. He finished his beer. "I don't know," he said finally.

"You don't know." Emphasizing his words, Mikhail tapped his steely forefinger on Alex's arm. "This be Mikhail's forty-five birthday. And you nutty bastard don't know what happens to my bubble!"

A small group of grinning Dravidians began to investigate about them. Carefully, they edged toward the three white men. Eyes wide, they leaned down towards the empty beer bottles.

With a thundering howl, Mikhail sprang up into the air, wildly waving his arms. The little men scattered like leaves in a wild wind. Some hid behind the copra loads; two dived overboard. Mikhail roared with laughter.

"What did they want?" Alex asked.

"They want bottles."

"Why not let them have them?"

"They too dirty," Mikhail answered, opening another for himself.

"I shouldn't think they'd mind. They can wash them."

Both men guffawed loudly. "No, no. Not bottles dirty. Men too dirty."

Bjorn laughed too.

I went over to the railing on the opposite side, as far away as possible, but so that I could still watch the loading. Three spotlights jetted their streams of light straight down the ship's white flank, spotlighting black figures as they moved in a long line across the green water, slowly paddling their little rafts piled high with copra. The small black dugouts crept constantly into sight, silhouetting ebony boatmen against the green brightness. The little vessels were usually two logs tied together with a small amount of wood carved out of the middle. The Dravidians who rowed them were naked and wet. They paddled with little effort, something in their uncorrupted time sense telling them they need not hurry.

This atavistic time sense was delightfully visible. Too often I felt like the white rabbit of Alice's Wonderland, always a little late, always a little desperate with the impending doom of it all. Space-time, I thought, is like riding in a taxi at rush hour: space swallowing time. But the Dravidians acted as if there would always be time.

What went on in their steaming jungle? I wondered. How did they live their gentle lives from day to day? What did their houses look like? Did the women smile and did the children play? My wanderlust was like a fever. Those tiny boats plowing their black paths through the darkness might take me to some wonderful thing. For who can know for sure where any search might lead?

The high-pitched voice of the first mate reached me.

"You, Savo! Report to Captain immediately!"

"I will not," Savo growled indignantly. "I am with friends." There was the sound of a bottle banged sharply on the deck. I went back to see what was happening. Alex was already standing.

"We're in the path of the monsoon," he said gently. "Maybe in danger. Go, Savo."

Mikhail also got up, unsteadily, stretching arms and scratching extensive middle.

"It is so dull up there," Savo moaned, still sprawled on deck.

"Monsoon," Alex reminded. "You might find an interesting message waiting."

"Oh, it is never interesting!" Savo said forlornly, slowly pulling himself upright. "I receive messages all the time. None is interesting."

The second mate snarled a command down the open hatch. From a darker patch in the shadows, three large sailors thumped onto the deck. They stood just outside the dish of light. No one looked at them.

Savo stood, weaving and bewildered. Gently, the sailors led him away.

"The captain is furious," Bjorn called down to Alex. "He is going to lock Savo in the brig until he is sober."

Alex looked up. "Savo won't mind. He makes slivovic from dirty sneakers."

"You are cruel man," Bjorn laughed. "Maybe he will ship him home."

"He can't. We'd have to use hand signals, you said. I thought he was going to ship your friend the third mate back."

"From Penang unless he promises no more intercourse with me."

"Did you find out anything interesting?" I asked Alex.

"Well, it looks like we're not stopping at Haiphong until the return voyage."

"Aha!" said Bjorn. "I already know this. The situation is bad there. Better to wait a few weeks, after we leave Japan. Did they speak about Indonesia? There they put an American family in prison, mother, father, and two teenage girls. Imagine two young girls in an Indonesian jail. Terrible."

I frowned. "Do you think it really happened?"

"But naturally. Why not?"

"It's full out war according to Savo. Communists are in control, so the crew feels safe about going there."

"Not that safe for us, then?" I said.

"There's something they're all anxious about," Alex added. "They're all waiting for it, the whole damned lot of them – I don't know what."

"Let's go below," I said after a moment, conscious of Bjorn's probing gaze on us.

He shook his head as at two idiot children.

24. PENANG

Bob Makes a Big Jump

The Jessenice was scheduled to deliver the cargo of copra and the smelly load of onions to Penang. Our dirty scrap iron shipment would be offloaded in Singapore, the cotton in Hong Kong. The air, stirred only by the fairly slow motion of the ship, was dank and hot.

"We will be in Penang in three days." I was on deck talking to Robin and Sally when Bjorn joined us to report the news with his usual authority. Arrival and departure times would nonetheless persist in being a subject of speculation.

The children were chasing Bob again, scampering up and down the steep ladder-stairs and across the decks.

"That's good," I said.

"You think it is good news?" He grinned. "But Malaysia is in big civil war!"

"Surely Penang is safe enough."

"Nowhere is safe in the east anymore, not for Americans. Not in war."

"We heard that the war is over, the British already pulling out," said Robin.

"Aha! *Oui!* The British are fleeing Malaysia! They have made a mess of it. And the Dutch are retreating from Indonesia. They, too, leave their colony in chaos."

"Short of immolation," I said, "something has to be done about the appalling poverty."

"*D'accord*, but tell this to the Vietcong when you are captured and held as spies! Or Alex as a smuggler as Captain accuses." He turned to look knowingly at Alex.

"What's your latest news on the war in Indonesia?" Robin also turned to Alex. "Have you heard anything?"

Alex shook his head. "I've heard we won't be stopping in Vietnam until the return journey, but I'm not betting on it."

"Our captain must stop there at some point," Bjorn assured us. "He was scheduled to deliver to Saigon. He is a brave man our captain. But now with you Americans coming in, he is safer sailing to Haiphong harbor. He has a very important shipment to deliver to the Vietcong."

"So you say," said Alex.

"Not me," Bjorn answered with a giggle, "the third mate. If I do not believe him, who can I believe?"

We arrived in Penang on schedule. The ship anchored in the steaming bay along with hundreds of other ocean-going vessels. Oversight of the port was British. As usual, our ship anchored furthest out. The passengers hung around the deck, waiting for the little flat-bottomed water-taxis called sampans to take us across the mirror-smooth bay to the city of Penang. It was already five o'clock, and orders were to be back by ten.

Bob had been helping the workers unload. Dirty and happy, he bounded up to us: "I'm saying goodbye here. I'm getting off now instead of at Singapore. I talked the chaps into letting me drive down with them. They can use a strong shoulder." His beard was bushier than before and he wore sandals in deference to the unknown.

"Do you know Malaysian?" I asked.

My tone was almost envious.

"Not much. We make do. They're friendly blokes."

Harold snorted, but I understood what Bob meant. I too sometimes found it easier to get along with friendly people in a strange tongue than with unfriendly people in my own language.

Bob turned to the three children. "It was a pleasure to know you, kids." He shook Robin's hand and hugged Sally. She had tears in her eyes.

"Take care of yourself, Bob."

"We'll meet again."

Bob leapt lightly down to the cargo deck. The passengers waved. He lifted one foot over the rail, about to jump into the barge of onions below.

"Come here!" A snarling command reverberated over the deck. Bob pivoted, spun by the captain's voice. He looked up. The captain stood motionless at the railing beside the other passengers, two guards behind him at the door, just out of Bob's sight.

Bob hesitated. I wanted to shout a warning, tell him to hurry, escape while he still could. But I remained frozen like the rest.

"Come here," the captain repeated, less aggressively. "I want to say goodbye."

Everyone watched uneasily. Bob shrugged. He signaled his Malay friends to wait a minute. Then, taking his usual shortcut over railings and up walls, he bounded gracefully back to shake hands. An official farewell.

"May I see your passport?" the captain asked smoothly.

"It's all been arranged with the port authorities, sir. I'm not asking for a refund on the ticket to Singapore. There's no need to trouble you."

"Let me see your passport."

Bob handed it to him in silence. The captain shuffled the pages icily. The two sailors came to stand by him. My stomach knotted. I could see what was coming as it un-scrolled in slow motion. Abruptly, the captain slipped Bob's passport into the inner pocket of his jacket. Bob jumped to grab it.

Too late. The two sailors had moved in front of their captain. There was no change of expression on their faces.

"I'll go anyway," Bob sounded winded.

"You won't get beyond the first checkpoint," the captain sneered.

"You stole my passport. I'll report you to the authorities."

"On board my ship I keep all the passports."

"Sir –"

"Your authorities," the captain continued, "will not care to believe the complaints of a barefoot, bearded boy."

Harold pushed up beside Bob.

"Captain," he said, his voice trembling with indignation, "we are free men, British subjects. You cannot keep this young man prisoner. Let him go with these natives if he is fool enough to."

The captain transferred his basilisk stare to Harold.

"He is on my manifesto. I will deliver him to Singapore." His cold voice rose commandingly. "You are all cargo as far as I am concerned. I am responsible for my cargo. I see that it all reaches its destination. Just like," he sniffed as he pointed down to the crew sweeping the smelly remains of onions off the forward deck, "like the onions. The rest of you have roundtrip tickets: I deliver you all to Rijecka." His ice-grey eyes settled on Bob and the Australians: "And you to Singapore. You all be warned."

He turned on his heels. The two bodyguards closed behind him. Nobody spoke. We looked anywhere but at each other. Arabella broke the silence.

"He's right, honey. The Malaysian peninsula is dangerous. There's a civil war going on, I understand. That's pretty serious, if you ask me. Maybe captain takes his role of big brother a bit too seriously, but he is taking good care of us."

As if to rub Arabella's image away, Bob wiped his eyes.

"I'm going to report him to the consulate!" Harold's voice quavered with outrage. "In the old days of the Empire it would have been gunboats to starboard, I assure you."

Bob went down by ladder to try to convey the news to his friends. He tripped and almost fell from the bottom rung, twisting his ankle as he did so. Limping, he made his way to the barge that clung to the side of the ship where he tried to explain to his new friends what had happened. But the complexities which he himself could neither accept nor understand were beyond his ability to communicate. In the stonier fields of human relations, clear language is needed. Bob didn't have it at his command, even in English.

The Malaysians waved goodbye, understanding only that he was not, after all, going to join them. Pushing past us, Bob retreated to his cabin.

Subdued, the rest of us prepared to go ashore, each finding our own little sampans from those that hovered about the ship. The boats were flat and shallow, steered and propelled by one oarsman with one long oar. Our pilot stood behind us like a Venetian gondolier, skimming the low yet gondola-like vessel across the smooth bay. He wore baggy brown trousers and a thick blue cotton shirt with a black wool vest that reached below the waist. With rhythmic motions, he deftly swung his long oar, threading us slowly through hundreds of ships large and small that anchored in Penang Bay. The dockside, now at the end of its busy day, was almost silent, almost deserted. It was hard to believe Malaysia was in the midst of war.

We headed toward a line of taxis. Each consisted of a wickerwork love-seat on wheels, pulled by an outsized tricycle which was pedaled by a steely-legged old man. Alex and Wyd got in one; Jeff and I in the other.

The two drivers smiled under their straw cone hats, their kindly faces like polished olive roots in the fast gathering shadows. We set off towards the temple.

The heat of the evening thickened and softened every sound. The heavy silence and warmth lulled our senses. We passed an occasional native, his long silk dress shimmering in the soft evening light, his face friendly. Sometimes he smiled, before blending into the shadows of dark side streets.

Cyclists stopped as we came to a busy thoroughfare. Yellow lights shone from food stores, filled with people doing last minute shopping for evening meals. We were deposited at a temple standing on the corner near the main intersection. Wide steps led up to a red porch-like entrance striped with golden columns. The temple's façade swarmed with large carved dragons, painted crimson and gold, which drifted atop their own shadows cast by dim light bulbs hidden in the folds of their dragon-bodies. The entrance was crowded with people slowly moving in and out: shoppers with their arms full, office workers on their way home, the poor and the rich, each stopping briefly, reverently to burn incense and give thanks for another day.

Inside, the smoke of innumerable joss sticks stung my eyes. Worshippers strolled around, talking quietly together. They seemed a little like athletes relaxing before the big game – in this case, prayer.

At least seven altars were hidden in a maze of rooms. What seemed to be feverish, befuddling fantasies were carved into numberless screens and altar pieces. Everything was painted in thunderous crimson and gold. Enormous jars, decorated with porcelain dragon-snakes and filled with sand, stood before each altar. The worshippers lit joss-sticks in handfuls – some sticks three feet long – setting them carefully in the sand then stepping back to watch the pungent smoke spiral upward, as they serenely chanted their prayers. There seemed also to be professional prayer-sayers, priests who for an offering of money, chanted the text correctly while the pious penitent stood by, looking a little foolish.

Light came from the flickering flames of a hundred candles. Smoke and candlelight danced together like wavering spirits. The fragrant mists coiled me unsuspectingly into their red and gold embrace. The dreamlike images began to seem clear and understandable. Like wind blowing the empty night streets clear and clean, the incense cleared my brain of the debris of doubt and distrust that cluttered it. My mind stopped trying to puzzle out the whys and hows and whens of it all. Floating through the chambers, lightheaded yet aware, I felt safe.

I let the children wander off to explore mysterious altars. Alex had already gone somewhere on his own. I leaned against a cool, stone pillar. Occasionally a priest smiled at me, as if he knew what was happening. Then he passed by, in elegant euphoria, on obscure errands of his own.

Across the stone flagged, dark aisle I was startled to see Bob. His wiry frame leaned towards a priest, making him an offering as if asking for a prayer. He spoke intimately, his bushy blond beard catching reflections from the candlelight. How had he managed to get ashore without his passport, I wondered. Surely the captain had not given him a pass? Looking out of the corner of my eyes, he became more clearly defined through the thick atmosphere. It was a trick I'd taught myself when I found that staring straight ahead tended to blur things.

Reaching into an inner pocket of his jacket, Bob handed something to the priest. It was a rapid transaction, yet I seemed to witness it in slow motion. Then I blinked and was no longer sure if the entire thing had happened. Bob was no longer there. The priest was chanting a prayer, his gaze set serenely on the smoking altar.

I opened my eyes wide, blurring the picture. I shook my head, trying to clear it of the heady incense that seemed to be making mush of my brain. I went over to where Bob had been. He was heading for a side exit.

I saw Alex and waved him over. "That's Bob over there," I said, pointing.

"Hey," Alex called, "Bob!"

The man did not turn around. Impulsively, I went after him. Catching up, I reached a sympathetic hand to touch his sleeve.

"Bob –" I began. He turned. My arm fell. This man wasn't Bob. But I knew him. He glared at me, then strode off. Disoriented, I went back to Alex. "It wasn't Bob. He was that bearded sailor from Jessenice, dressed like Bob."

"Let's get the kids," Alex said immediately.

With Jeff and Wyd, we retraced our way outside. The evening air was fresh and made me feel almost cold. There's a war on, I remembered. The thought triggered rockets of old experience: early childhood in the Spanish Civil War, being a teen-ager in Europe during World War II.

On the temple steps I described to Alex what I'd seen the sailor do.

"Do you have any idea what he could be up to?" I asked.

"It could be a number of things."

"Like what?"

"It could be as simple as changing currency. Black market. Or it could be as serious as passing stolen documents."

"Or, drugs I suppose. The crew is technically aboard ship; only passengers are supposedly off, although we know Bob's been kept aboard. If this man does anything wrong, suspicion will land on poor Bob."

We made our way down the wide flight of stairs to the street.

"Is that sailor acting for the captain or on his own?" I wondered out loud.

"I would think he's at least acting with the captain's knowledge,"

"We're supposed to be back by ten. We'll be late again."

Nervously we shepherded our little family into our two waiting rickshaws. We moved down a long, black, empty avenue edged with a border of even blacker trees.

The kids had been bewitched by the temple. Now they sat as in a trance. The city delicately gave away small secrets as we headed back to port: a light in a little window, an unfamiliar smell from a darkened doorway, a soft sound. Small secrets that gave away nothing.

As we rounded the warehouse by the dock, Wyd's sleepy eyes widened in astonishment. "Look!" she exclaimed.

We were altogether unprepared for the phosphorescent surprise of light and fire spread across the bay. Every vessel floated on a carpet of blue-green phosphorescent light. This cold fire splashed and licked up along their iron anchor chains. A splash, a ripple immediately turned incandescent in the warm night. In the black between the ships, tiny sampans spun to and fro, sparkling like spit-dragons on the Fourth of July.

In addition, all the ships in the harbor, and there were hundreds of them, from all the seagoing nations, had turned on their finest display of harbor lights. Military vessels were the most lavish: symmetrical and elegant at the same time. Sometimes small lights outlined an entire warship. One had strung bulbs around each porthole. Cruise ships were the most inventive, with multicolored bulbs dangling in decorative patterns from their decks. Freighters were not to be outdone, though. They too had lights strung around their funnels, and brilliant spotlights splashing their still busy holds. Tugs, yachts, sailboats, tenders, all did their very best to add to the gala display.

We were mesmerized.

Jeff broke the spell. "There's our sampan," he pointed, responding to a wave from the owner.

As we boarded the little craft, cool flames brushed our feet. Magically our sampan glided from shore on its own carpet of fire. I was glad we had read about flying carpets as we floated by the Continent with No Name.

Now we slid under the prows of great ships, including many old acquaintances from other ports. From our low perspective, we gazed far up their iridescent sides, which rose like steely cliffs out of the flaming froth.

It took well over an hour to reach our freighter, and yet the long ride was far too short for all of us. The boatman, too, seemed entranced by the glorious spectacle. It was obviously not a regular event. He did not try to hurry. Rhythmically dipping his oar into the black water, he brought it up overflowing with sparks. Doing the same with their fingers, the children poured their own cascades of fireworks. One by one the giant ships turned off their ostentatious light-displays as their passengers and crews arrived safely aboard. Eventually only the Jessenice, as usual the furthest out, was still lit up.

"If there wasn't a war on, Penang would have been a wonderful place to jump ship," I said, dreamily.

"Sssh!" Alex whispered, bringing me quickly back to reality.

The instant that the boatman caught hold of the gangplank's railing the lights above went out. Darkness pressed down on the harbor like a cloud, leaving only thin wedges of cold fire between blackness of air and black water. Alex led the way up the slippery steps. I was last. I waited for the sampan to shove off then leaned dangerously over to splash one final watery fountain of light before climbing to the gloom above.

As I reached the others on deck, I glimpsed the shadowy figure of Stefan fluttering out of sight.

Departure, we were told next morning at breakfast, was imminent. As soon as off-loading was complete, the ship must leave, so no day-passes for anyone. Harold was livid at being prevented from reaching the British Consulate, where he'd wanted to lodge a complaint for Bob.

It was sunset before the last, wide, flat barge was heaped high with the last of our scrap-iron shipment and preparations for departure were begun. I went to the forward deck to watch the familiar routine. The rest of the passengers were there, standing side by side but separate, gazing at the pretty scene. The sun was like a red circle at the narrow end of a long funnel. Eagles flew in the golden mid-distance.

Once the ship was out to sea, we expected Bob to come out of his cabin and join us as usual. But he refused.

"I take him meals," Stefan told me the next day, anxious. "But he refuse. I leave trays outside his door, but he does not open the door even after I go."

"Maybe he'll talk to the children," I suggested.

But Bob could not bring himself to answer their cheerful calls through his door.

This upset Jeff and Wyd.

"Isn't it typical," I said to Alex, "after all our efforts to protect them from the obvious ill-will on board this ship, it has to be good-natured, lovable Bob who louses things up."

"Hardly very seriously."

"I don't mean it's serious. I simply mean that Bob unintentionally succeeded in hurting them, where none of the others have managed to."

"The kids will get over it."

"That's not my point. Bob thinks he's accomplishing something by acting indignant and upset. He thinks there's something special about expecting the world to behave decently."

"I'd say he did not expect the world to behave badly."

"In either case, he should be out running the decks and jumping up walls, singing at the top of his lungs."

"Is that what you'd do?" Alex smiled.

I paused in my pacing. "I don't know what I would do. That's why I'm on this journey. I wonder, though. I think it would annoy the captain to see Bob laughing and singing as if he didn't give a damn about what happened. He wants us crushed and miserable – it makes us easier to push us around. Why play into his hands?"

I lay down with Alex, feeling the steady, forward-pull of the freighter. Now that we had off-loaded the scrap iron and load of onions, the ship sailed higher on the water, and responded more actively to even small changes in wave patterns: forward, a fast side to side, and then down, a bounce up, and so on.

Everyone has a job to do, I mused, but no one knows how to do it until after the job is done. No wonder things are such a mess. I thought of the children. Everything had conspired to coddle them, protect them, as life had obviously coddled Bob. But if Bob had not been coddled, would he have been courageous and strong enough to brave the adventures of the world in the first place?

I had no desire to get rid of that, any more than Alex did. We did not wish to toughen the children so they learned to put a constricting shell around themselves. We wanted to strengthen something else; strengthen some other part so that they would sing for joy at the challenges they met in life. Strengthen them inwardly, so they could become heroes in their own lives, examples themselves.

Ideologies don't help. Fixed ideas often take over. People with fixed ideas never let go for a minute. They hold them fast, swinging them like truncheons, using them like flame-throwers. And if someone responds with another, different idea, they feel threatened. I didn't want my children to be like that. I wanted to keep them free from fear-induced ideologies.

After a while I said: "Anyway, I hope Wyd and Jeff never react to challenges as limply as Bob did this time."

Bob did not speak to any of the passengers again. With the captain's permission, he slipped off unseen at Singapore. Much to Jeff and Wyd's sadness, the Australians disembarked, too.

25. STRAITS OF MALACCA

Bumps

The ocean had been blue for days. It was as much made of color as of wetness and light. I thought it would be nice to be an ocean. Instead of being merely thick grey surges, I could imagine myself being made of colors: colors which might mix or stay apart but always be light, fluid, translucent.

My hands stuck to a film of soot and sun oil on the stair railing. A cylinder of sweet oily odor floated down from the sundeck. At the top of the stairs, almost blocking passage from the cabin deck below, Bjorn lay strewn like a wet bandana over his deckchair. His bikini, which could not get shorter around the thighs, had gotten shorter around his glistening stomach.

"Hi, Bjorn." I stepped around him heading for a place at the railing outside the line of acrid funnel exhaust.

Stiff as a seagull, Harold landed at the railing nearby, just beyond talking distance. His quartz eyes gazed at our wake undulating a foaming line through the early afternoon calm.

He hopped closer. "I've had enough! If you continue to speak to that bloody Dane, you can't speak to me."

I sighed.

"If that man insults me once more I'll hit him," Harold seethed. His stiff frame shook with anger. "I swear I will. His bloody silver forehead be damned!"

Harold's nature had congealed. He had been born into the unbreakable British class system where each person is given a shield of decorum, sugar coating for the bitter pill of being, in this case, working class. In exchange, Harold had sacrificed the arms of a man. How many times, I wondered, had his ear been boxed, his arm roughly pulled, his bottom smacked by parents nervously pushing him to the safe haven of propriety. He had landed there, proper as hell, and ever since been terrified to move, until his arms had dropped off, and he could no longer hug.

"You're making this kind of awkward," I said. "I mean, we're all in the same boat. We've got to try to get along."

"One must observe the rules of proper conduct," he growled.

I patted his arm and turned to leave, then hesitated when I saw Bjorn.

"I understand you, Jane!" Bjorn called over, waving his bottle of suntan lotion. "You talk to the very young and the very old." He grinned at Harold. "You are curious about everything. It does not matter what. Like me in manu-are."

Harold reddened angrily. I squeezed past Bjorn's deck chair onto the stairs.

"You can tell Alex!" Harold spoke across Bjorn's oily body. "If either of you talks to that bastard, I won't answer for the consequences! And that goes for the children!"

He turned abruptly and I watched him walk along the deck, taking the long way around to his cabin. His compact body pressed against the freshening wind. At the forward end he disappeared down the ladder-stairs: first his short bowlegs with their wide flannel trousers flapping, then his straight back, until finally all I could see were a few long strands of hair streaming away from the back of his head.

I went on down.

"Hello," Alex said, coming up beside me as I reached the cabin deck.

"Hello." I put my arms around him. We hugged for a moment, then wandered back to our cabin where we collapsed on a bed, talking quietly, welcoming the more regular motion of waves as we neared the open Pacific.

"I had another talk with Savo this morning," Alex said. "According to him, Bjorn's been smuggling drugs from one end of the equator to the other for quite some time. You name the place, he's got it covered. He's an addict and so's Grace, but she doesn't have the tumor."

"That explains…. the story about his tumor, is that made up?"

"No. Apparently, he really does have that."

"And drugs to prevent it from growing?"

"Well, yes, those too. They all work at killing the pain."

"Citizens of the world, Bjorn says, but the two of them just go from ship to ship, hardly ever landing."

"That makes him a lot less sinister than I imagined."

"True. He may drive us crazy, but he's probably not dangerous."

"He's driving Harold crazy." I told him of Harold's warning not to talk to Bjorn.

"That's ridiculous."

"Bjorn is so infuriating, though – I sympathize with Harold."

"I'm not going to worry about it," Alex said. "Anyway, who needs Harold?"

"That's how I feel," I answered, stretching. "Who needs any of them?"

Just then a horrible shriek pierced our ears.

It was followed by a man's shout, then a cry from Wyd. In a flash I was out the door, running towards the sound, Alex on my heels. Stefan was already ahead of us.

Jeff lay screaming on the dining room floor. Wyd was crying as she stared down at his writhing form. Harold hovered nearby. Stefan quickly knelt beside him.

"What happened?" I gasped.

"He hit his head," Harold said defensively.

"Careful. May be concussion," Stefan said.

"I was showing him how to do a somersault and he fell," said Harold.

"On his head," I raged. "With 20,000 tons of ship coming up as he went down."

"Take it easy, Jane," Alex picked up the screaming child and carrying him in his arms, Alex strode to the children's cabin. We all followed. Carefully Alex placed him on his bunk. Jeff began to vomit. A bump appeared over his right temple. It kept growing.

"Mummy, I can't see you."

"It's okay, Jeff. I'm here." I lay down beside him.

Stefan and Harold hovered at the door.

"Isn't there a doctor on board?" Alex asked.

"No doctor," said Stefan. "But I have a special powder that will help."

"I'm sorry, Jane," Harold said, still belligerent. "I didn't do it on purpose."

Wyd took Alex's hand.

"There must be a doctor," I said. "Stefan, someone acts as doctor on board."

Stefan shook his head. "Trust me," he said. "I have medicine."

"The children certainly stump around by themselves enough," Harold said.

"No one accused you of anything," Alex said.

"I say, you're taking it a bit poorly, aren't you?"

"For God's sake," I interrupted. "What happens when a sailor's injured?"

Stefan hesitated. "The first mate. But he sleeps now. When he wakes I ask him to look at Jeff."

"He's going to look at Jeff now," Alex said.

Stefan bowed his head. "Yes, Mister, I go call him."

Harold left, too.

"We'd better keep him awake," advised Alex. "If it's concussion he'd better not go to sleep."

I wrapped Jeff in a warm blanket then sat in the armchair, propping him upright in my arms to help keep him awake.

"I can't see you, Mummy."

"You'll be fine in just a bit. I'm right here."

Jeff's eyes kept closing, his head drooping onto his chest and my shoulder. We went on talking to him. Twenty long minutes later Stefan knocked on the door. He was followed by the first mate who strode into the room still buttoning his fly. He looked at Jeff in my arms and grunted.

The bump was a good two inches high by now. Without a word to any of us, he took out an oversized clasp knife from his pants pocket. It was about ten inches long. I gasped. He leaned towards the little boy. We watched. Everything was moving in slow motion.

"What are you doing?" Alex said.

"What?" cried Jeff, hearing the anxiety. I could feel him stiffen.

The first mate said nothing. He leaned closer. The knife was three inches from the bump. I imagined Jeff, fuzzy and trusting, with the blade pressed to his temple. I imagined his pain. I imagined damage if there were cracks in the skull.

Two inches.

I screamed. The same instant, Alex grabbed the mate's arm.

Angry, the mate shook him off.

"You were going to press it down?" Alex demanded.

"That's what we do for sailors."

"Skip it. He's not a sailor."

"Why you wake me if you no want me?" the first mate growled. He pushed Alex aside and left.

Stefan closed the door behind him, waiting.

Jeff's sight had begun to return. "How many fingers do you see?" Alex asked him, holding up one finger.

Jeff gave it some thought: "Four."

Alex looked at me.

"I have the powder," Stefan said quietly. "You take my word. It really work. Please try it."

"Okay, Stefan," Alex said. "We'll try it. Thank you."

Stefan carefully unwrapped a brown paper bag and spooned out some white powder into a glass of warm water. When it was dissolved, he soaked a bandage in it. Then he very gently placed the bandage on Jeff's forehead. Deftly, he wrapped a dry one over it to keep it in place.

"It will take away the swelling," he assured us. "In half hour I change bandage."

We waited anxiously after he left, listening to Wyd talk quietly to Jeff. When Stefan returned he took off the bandage. The swelling had gone down. Only a little, but down, nonetheless. The lurid knob had softened, whitened.

"You see, it works." Stefan spoke gently as he fixed a new bandage in place. "The sailors all try to come to me first. Because I have the powder." He added modestly. "They do not like the first mate to take care."

"I can see why," Alex said. His voice was still gruff, but his eyes were grateful.

"Change bandages every half hour to midnight," Stefan said. "You need me, you call me."

I pressed his hand.

The afternoon wore on. Around four Stefan quietly brought us tea and cookies. When evening closed in, Alex took Wyd into dinner; I did not leave Jeff. Stefan brought a tray to the cabin. Under his watchful eye, I changed the bandages. When Alex and Wyd came back after dinner, Wyd got into bed and read herself to sleep. Alex stayed on, chatting. Finally, about midnight, we stopped trying to keep Jeff awake and tucked him in, too.

"He's only sleeping," Alex comforted me.

"Yes."

"The swelling does seem to have gone way down."

"Yes, it has."

191

Alex went next door to our cabin. I sat beside Jeff's bed, wide awake and afraid. Every so often I leaned over to listen to his breathing. To listen that there was breathing.

I jerked awake when Alex came in at dawn the next morning.

"He hasn't woken up yet," I said.

Alex put a hand on Jeff's forehead, then took his wrist. "His pulse seems okay. Stefan's on his way. Why don't you have a shower and put on something cool?"

"I don't know..."

"Go on. I'll stay here."

Reluctantly, I went next door. The quick shower made me feel better. Drying my hair, I looked suddenly over to the open porthole. Bjorn was gazing in solicitously.

"The poor boy." He whispered loudly. "You are lucky. Someone tried to kill me too. If that happened to me I'd be dead. But don't worry. I'm on your side."

He popped his head out and disappeared.

26. EAST CHINA SEA

Chinese Junks

The fuzziness in Jeff's head took six long, anxious days to clear. We kept him in bed. Stefan's attentive ministrations allayed our fears somewhat. He hovered about, bringing occasional treats, tidying the room, talking about the goings on aboard the ship, noting the change in the weather.

"Keep warm, Missus," he would warn me, tucking Wyd's scarf into her jacket before an outing. "It be winter, now. Winds, and very slippery." To Wyd he admonished: "Hold Mummy's hand, you understand?"

Our next stop would be Hong Kong, where we had a friend. Stan Karnow was Time Magazine's Bureau Chief there. "He'll know of a doctor who will check on Jeff," Alex assured me. "And we'll also get his advice about whether we should continue on to Japan on this crazy ship. He'll give us the political scoop about what's really happening out here."

Storms hunched over us, grey and grumpy. Rough waves shoved the Jessenice into the northern swirls of winter. Vietnam lay somewhere off to port, walled away by mists. We watched giant wind-frothed waves creating exquisite spirals and curls at the tops of massive mountains of water. Wet curves and circles of white and blue tunnels, which I had thought were a peculiarly enchanting Asiatic artist's vision, now swirled into chilly motion, putting us unexpectedly into the picture as if we were in an Oriental ink-drawing.

Chinese junks frisked about the ship like Pekingese puppies around a white Russian wolfhound. Doubtless they had kept a watchful eye on the comings and goings within their waters for centuries, catching odd bits of information along with their silver fish. Their miniscule craft were like toys on the rowdy seas of a very rough battle in a bathtub. Only their dumpy shape kept them from being swamped. High poops and wide, rounded bottoms bobbed them to the tops of watery cliffs. Twirled by snowy gusts of spume, they tipped at impossible angles, sliding inside tunnels, then zipping out to escape crushing tons of water. They were home to whole families. We could hardly conceive how.

Now that we were in the Orient, I concentrated the children's studies on things Oriental but kept current affairs out of our talk. Despite the rhetoric, in my experience, wars and revolutions remained the same through space and time. People with everything to lose against people with nothing to lose. Love, laughter, food, family, against more than enough money. Then there are those who merely love to exert authority over the more vulnerable. Our captain was such a one. No give, no quarter. Instead rules, regulations, directives and authority. Others like Stefan preferred kindness and fair play even in unfair situations. Perhaps the captain had had that impulse once long ago when he had come to Stefan's rescue. But he may have had to pay too high a price for his memorable act of empathy. Society tends to give those with a special impulse to goodness a hard time.

Meantime my children would have their fill of their own wars as they grew older, since nothing basic had changed in the world as yet. Meantime, I wanted to give them grounds for the strength of their own adult choices later on, and was grateful for Stefan's special concern for Jeffy in this emergency.

As Jeff healed, we took him out onto the chilly deck for short walks in the fresh air. Afterwards, back on our bunks, noses tickling into warmth, enjoying the roller-coaster effect of the China Sea, the children listened happily to the stories Alex loved to tell:

One day the Stone Monkey went to the Buddha.

'I am now the Great Sage Equal to Heaven,' he proclaimed. 'By rights I should have the Throne of the Jade Emperor!'

Buddha looked at him in a kindly way and replied: 'The Jade Emperor was there long before you were born. You are still shucking your animal form, while the Jade Emperor wears his years like a crown. Imagine a crown studded with thousands of diamonds: each diamond is a thousand thousand years. That is the crown of the Jade Emperor.'

'I don't see that it matters when he started,' replied Stone Monkey rudely. 'By right of my great intellectual powers the Throne is mine!'

The Buddha nodded. 'If you can jump off my hand you can have the Throne of the Jade Emperor of Heaven.'

'It's agreed!' Monkey shouted.

Climbing onto the Buddha's palm, he grabbed his air trapeze and somersaulted off into the great unknown. Tumbling across vast distances, he finally came to five pillars. They glowed pink in the last rays of light from Buddha's wise old eye.

"This is the end of the Universe!' Monkey exulted. He stopped to pee at the base of one of the pillars. On another he inscribed these words: 'Great Sage Equal to Heaven'. Then impudently riding his air trapeze, he summer-salted back.

'Give me the Throne of the Jade Emperor,' he shouted on his return.

'Oh, no,' sighed the gentle Buddha. 'You have not left my hand.'

'You're crazy!' cried Monkey. 'I reached the very edge of the universe!'

195

'Look,' said the Buddha, and pointed to his fourth finger. Astonished, Monkey read: 'Great Sage Equal to Heaven.' And as he read he could not help but smell monkey pee.

'There is so much to learn,' sighed the Buddha as he gently pushed the Stone Monkey out of the West Gate of Heaven.

* **

The oriental side of the children's humanity was tickled by the wry humor. The Laughing Buddha laughed with them and made them laugh. Because such good effort had been put into the try, they did not feel shamed, but ready to go at it again.

We found the Seeker to be the real hero of Asiatic lore. Sometimes disreputable, sometimes irreverent, often improbably humble, the Seeker wanders his hard way, peacefully upsetting all the usual values. Sometimes he simply sits and waits, like an empty cup ready to be filled. Sometimes he drifts, like leaves of autumn across a garden path, making the path more beautiful. When he stumbles across a sleeper, sometimes he wakes him. Sometimes he doesn't.

The Seeker might be dirty, thirsty, laughing, dancing, begging, or simply meditating, but he is always wide open to immediate experience. And he doesn't ever explain what a "right action" actually is.

We probed, imagined, and talked over new ideas. We dreamed through reproductions of Chinese ink drawings and Japanese prints. We told Chinese legends. We applied ourselves to puzzling Zen koans:

"What will you do when there is nothing to do?"

"Once you get to the top of a hundred foot pole, how can you climb higher?"

"If you were hanging by your teeth from a branch that stretched out over a terrifying abyss, and in your hands you held beloved treasures, and to your feet you had tied more treasures, then your Zen Master came along and asked 'What is Zen?' what would you do?"

The strangeness of it all did not trouble the children, partly because they had gotten used to strange things, partly because there is something natural when everything is strange and wonderful.

Later, standing out on our deck, in the lee of the wind by myself, wearing my thick goats' wool sweater from Delos, the Island upon which the Sun God Apollo had been born, I wondered about Vietnam hidden over the waves on our port side. That would have been a wonderful stop. Thick, shiny, green rubber jungles offering work; silver rice paddies mirroring the forms of clouds like ghosts in antique mirrors, while feeding millions well; a graceful, sophisticated Saigon, one of the most cosmopolitan cities in the Orient. I knew little about any of it, but still I imagined myself walking Saigon's elegant wide avenues, congested with pedestrians and bicycle-carts, its intriguing sounds and tantalizing aromas unfolding and enfolding around me, as alluring, unfamiliar sights tempted me to absorb a new culture.

"If you were a teacher in the States you wouldn't last a week," Arabella had come up beside me. She, too, was bundled against the chilly winds. "Where on earth do you pick up what you tell your children?"

"Hello, Arabella."

"Stone monkeys," she went on, smiling. "Air trapezes. It's crazy, Honey. It's just crazy. Wyd told me your Stone Monkey story over a game of 'Sorry'."

"You think I should teach them about the cloud trapezes of modern technology instead?" I said.

"Oh, honey. You're such a tease."

A chunky junk climbed precariously up the inner face of a blue wave curling as high as our passenger deck. Slipping sideways in a sort of loop, it hung upside down in the glass smooth upward thrust, then burst through the whirling white foam at the very top edge to slide down the outer face. Almost instantly another powerful blue curve of water raised it to phenomenal heights. It was near enough for me to see inside to its tiny kitchen. Everything was tightly locked down. Nothing spilt, nothing moved out of place, not even the shiny tea-kettle on the stove. The inside floor, ceiling and walls seemed to be rounded like the inside of a balloon. An acrobat, himself, the

197

fisherman walked whichever side kept him upright. The boat's motor was modern, strong.

A new fishing boat suddenly appeared to port side, twirling up into the wave's spume topping. Two tall, firmly-braced steel antennae spoke of the new universe of modern technology. When the tug-like boat came skillfully out from under crashing tons of water into clear view, I saw elaborate modern radio equipment such as we carried, which the two steel antennae should have prepared me for.

"Jeff and Wyd may not know much about science yet," I said, "at least, not out of their own experience. But I think they understand something of the Jade Emperor's way. And the Jade Emperor will make science a more comprehensible subject."

"What on earth is the Jade Emperor's way?"

"How can I explain it? When we were living on a mountainside in Greece we could tell the moment that olive-picking time had come around again. The first rain-cloud in September was all the sign we needed. We'd use our car to drive our Greek mountain friends to their olive groves down in the plain for the harvest. They'd all understood the Jade Emperor's message. I mean, none of us had a telephone, let alone television, but we'd know when and where to meet: the day, the time – everything."

"Do you really expect any of that to help the children get along in the States? We do have telephones, you know."

"I'm trying to strengthen something else inside them, even if it's not practical. Something transcendent that matters too."

"Besides," Alex pointed out later when I repeated what Arabella had said, as we lay safely on our bunks, rocking to the wild winds and waves, waiting for the children to ring the gong for lunch. "Anybody can learn to use the phone."

27. HONG KONG

Uneasy Splendor

L ate one night we cast anchor in Hong Kong's jittery, glittery harbor. The next morning, suspicious British port authorities boarded the ship in force. They proceeded to attack the cargo of cotton from Karachi like a plague of bole weevils. One in every ten bales was split open for search, whereupon it puffed up to four times its pressure-packed size, spilling fluff into the winds. The customs inspectors stabbed their soft whiteness with long sharp knives. Caught by the cold wind, cotton wafted over the steely frame of the ship until everything was lightly layered with white fuzz. The usually impassive officers, usually spic and span in their blue winter suits, were now blurred by cotton, and rigid with irritation.

Wrapped warmly, ready to go ashore as soon as passports cleared, we took our usual place at the railing on second deck. Sturdy junks attached themselves to the ship's flanks, eight or nine to a slippery side.

The junks were homes to extended families, which both lived and worked on them. Their high poops were painted in bright colors and decorated with curly-queues of oriental fantasy. The poop decks housed galleys and sleeping quarters which swarmed with activity in the furry fog. Below, the extremely deep holds were being packed with our cargo. Domestic routine continued, uninterrupted by the Jessenice's off-loading of cotton. Ancient grandmothers cooked unperturbed on deck while the more able-bodied members pitched into the heavy work of stacking bales into compact piles in deep holds. Tiny-eyed tots waved gaily from papoose position on the backs of hardworking mothers. Five and six-year-olds played their games with easy unconcern for crane-heavy loads that zeroed in on their miniscule homes. Some of the smallest children were attached to long ropes tied to their middles at one end and at the other to the gaily-painted galley doors. Aside from this, there was no sign of worry at this dangerous and very public life. There was no bickering tone, no irritated family squabbling. They worked hard and laughed a lot.

By mid-afternoon the passengers and crew had been cleared through passport control and customs. It had all been done politely but slowly in the lounge. We all piled into an open motor launch to go ashore. The Jessenice had anchored far from the harbor's head, and it was a long, chilly ride. But beautiful. The launch threaded its way through mists wrapped like the hands of giant ghosts around the hundreds of colorful boats dotting the harbor: houseboats, tubby tugs, black barges, junks, and our many old freighter friends – ships plying the same long route as the Jessenice. Behind us in the soft fog, our cotton-fluffed freighter loomed like a white swan over her brood of baby vessels. After a while she blended into the white air and disappeared.

Ahead lay the "Jewel of the Orient." We wandered the steep streets, under skyscrapers that shadowed the multiplicity of the market place and all the varieties of poverty and misery – and riches, too. There was something oddly familiar about Hong Kong. Like meeting a stranger with a broken leg, when yours is broken too.

"Let's take a back way through the market," I said. "I think it will be different."

The market stretched across small alleyways and up steep slopes. "This is the Hill of the Dragon," Alex told the children. "It's very bad luck to disturb the dragon. That's why it hasn't been built up like the rest of Hong Kong."

Wyd looked around for the dragon.

"A real dragon?" Jeff asked dubiously.

"Yes, in its way," Alex said. "You can find it by its force-field."

Wyd stopped trying to see it.

"How can you feel it?" Jeff wanted to know.

"One way is by putting your hands out. They'll tingle all the time you're over the dragon's lair," Alex explained.

"My hands tingle!" Wyd said, delighted.

"Then we're over the dragon's lair!" Alex said.

Wyd and Jeff walked ahead with hands outstretched. But soon the sights of the bustling, noisy, fragrant market streets engrossed them so that they forgot to feel for the dragon's power.

Hungry at last, we found a restaurant in a drab, three storey building, already filled almost to overflowing with hungry businessmen. We ascended through noisy, crowded, undecorated rooms until on the windowless top floor we found an empty table. Waiting for service, we heard a sonorous chant.

A white-aproned youth came in with a tray of steaming, covered dishes. He was chanting his menu in Chinese. At Alex's signal, he paused by our table to set down four small covered dishes. He was followed by a girl carrying another tray. Sometimes four youths at once would be sing-songing their wares to the musical background chorus of luncheon talk. The Chinese language engulfed us in its musical complexity. Its tunefulness compensated for our being unable to fathom it. Before long our table was filled with bubbling bowls giving off enticing odors.

"What's in them?' Jeff asked.

"I have no idea," I said. "But it smells great. Do you know, Alex?"

"Well," he said, examining the menu. "Once of these is fungi. Hopefully they mean mushrooms. Then there could be Japanese sea-moss steamed and stuffed. I want to try the vegetarian goose."

"Do you think he's made of vegetables?" I asked.

"I think it was his diet," Alex answered solemnly. "Because there be also a vegetarian shark-fin soup listed."

"I bet there be seaweed," I said.

"I bet there be rice," Wyd added, laughing with me.

"I bet there be soy sauce," Jeff said, grinning.

There was no way of telling what most dishes consisted of. We could smell and if we liked the sweet, the pungent, the delicate fish aromas, we'd go ahead and taste. Even if we didn't particularly like the smell at first, we usually tried the dish anyway.

Alex was anxious to contact Stan Karnow, so while we ate he went off to find a telephone.

Wyd and Jeff faced the challenge of chopsticks. A nearby Chinese family giggled in a friendly way at their struggles. Without speaking, their four children pantomimed how to hold the sticks in one hand, while moving them about like pincers.

Then to eat.

They lifted some mouth-sized bits from the main dishes in the middle of the table and placed them artistically on their plates. Then they lifted them carefully into their open mouths. As Jeff and Wyd automatically began to imitate the smooth, effective gestures, they became proficient in the new skill. Of course there was spilling and laughter, as much at the Chinese table as at ours. From their beaming faces I could tell that Jeff and Wyd felt they were among friends.

"Stan was unexpectedly called away on assignment," Alex said slipping back into his chair. "He won't be back for another three days."

"We'll be gone."

We went on eating.

"Do you think the British know something we don't about our ship?" I broke the silence.

"It seems as though they were looking for something in particular, didn't it?"

Alex nodded, thinking about something else. He put down his chopsticks and took slow sips of his green tea.

I waited.

"How would you feel about jumping ship here?" he said, his voice low. "I could cable Time, Life, and Sports Illustrated, courtesy of Stan, for free-lance assignments in this part of the world. I'm not sure it's wise to go on with this mystery voyage."

"Not go back to the boat at all?"

"That's right."

For a moment I thought of the children's gorgeous scrapbooks, the Hungarian puppets, all our clothes. We had brought everything with us from Greece that we owned and wanted to keep. We had decided to put nothing in storage, but instead to give away everything we would not be taking. It would leave us freer, we'd told the kids.

"How about trying to wait for Japan?" I suggested. "It's closer."

Alex laughed.

"Closer. That's thinking, darling. We could fly back."

"That's what I mean, if we keep going straight ahead."

When we emerged from the restaurant the winter afternoon had closed in. The cold had, too. Gaudy lights lit the damp streets. Offices were emptying. The children were tired. We made our way to the harbor, found the launch to take us back to the ship, and sped out into the winter dusk.

Seen from the launch, Hong Kong was pure splendor. Fuzzed by a light mist, a million lights shimmered in the vaporous dark. Skyscrapers and massed shanties rose to create incandescent mountains along its edges, shimmering colorful reflections into the black waters below. Thousands of sailing craft wrinkled the harbor surface, signaling their presences by means of furry golden beams. Cruise boats glittered close to the harbor's head, where the warmth of the city dispelled the curling mists. There the calm waters reflected pink, purple, and orange neon calligraphs, some as much as three stories high. The squiggly signs buzzed off and on, below and above, backwards and forwards, in flashy neon magnificence.

From a darker part of the shore, explosions of shattered light suddenly burst into the sky. Sky rockets flowered into purple and pink, burning fleetingly and leaving their dark images on the night.

Then more and more followed.

"What's that?" Jeff asked.

"It looks like a fireworks factory caught fire," Alex said.

Our eyes followed the ziggy strokes and gaudy arcs of flares and sparks that looked like Chinese writing in the sky. They still streaked the sky when we reached our ship and we stayed on deck for a while, watching in wonder until the last fiery rocket splashed its green and purple light against the black sky.

Even then I didn't send the children to bed. The ship was readying for departure, and I understood the still strange thrill of leaving port. Creaks of undecipherable sorts, slapping of waves, crashes of workmen's tools. One last junk pulled softly away. Last bits of cotton were swept up as holds clanged shut. The two giant anchor chains thundered aboard.

Silently, the ghostly ship slipped away towards the open sea. Shadowy vessels drifted noiselessly by. Foghorns hooted.

"What do you think is going on with the ship, then?" I asked Alex, too quietly for the children to hear.

"It may have something to do with what we're carrying. The port authorities here obviously expected to find something."

"Any idea what? More explosives?"

"All the passengers knew about the explosives. It's more likely they were half-being used as a cover for something else the ship is smuggling. Whatever it is, we'll jump ship in Japan."

Clustered like devils in the cold black of their fog-colored bridge, the captain and officers twisted the Jessenice through the small islands outside the harbor. One last narrow stretch, and Hong Kong in all its uneasy splendor was wiped off the blackboard.

28. FORMOSA

The Secret

"We're going to have a secret," I said at lessons the next morning. "It's a very important secret. No one else must know about it except the four of us: you two, me and Daddy."

"Not Stefan?" asked Wyd.

I shook my head. Especially not Stefan. For his sake.

"What is the secret?" asked Jeff.

"The secret is that we're not going back to Rijecka on the boat. We're going to get off in Japan and go on to America from there."

America! Their eyes widened with wonder. The ins and outs of why this should be a secret did not concern the children. Wyd was reading Enid Blyton's Secret Five adventures, so she understood the importance of secrets – all kinds of secrets. Her face shone as Jeff went over to the great globe on top of the dresser.

"Okay," he said, examining it. "Tell me where we're going."

Given the names of the places, he traced our probable route. We were passing the Pescadores Islands off the southern end of the big strategic island of Formosa, which lay to starboard. Red China, as we called it, was not far to port. We would continue north through the stormy Formosa Straits and on through the Inland Sea to Osaka. Forsaking the ship there, we'd go to ancient Nara, proceed to Tokyo, and then:

"We go east to America?" Jeff exclaimed. "Why do people call it West?"

"I guess they haven't been all the way around the world as we have. They don't yet know there isn't any east or west. Just a little wet round globe. Do you know, that if we fly over the Pacific Ocean we'll pass the International Date-line. When it's Tuesday here, it's Wednesday in America. It means that with jets you can travel fast enough to leave America on Wednesday and get to Japan on Tuesday."

It took the rest of the lesson to explain. I set a lamp so it shone directly onto the globe like a sun. Turning the globe in the lamp's rays, I showed how the sun "rises" each morning. Night and day were seen in miniature and imagined in real.

"Who invented the line?"

"Why did they put it there?"

"Then Monday or Tuesday isn't really real," Wyd pondered. "If it can be turned around like that, it isn't real."

"Well, there's other things real about them. They come one after another as people named them. Like months."

They pondered for a while, studying the globe.

"Since we have a secret," I said, "what shall we do with it?"

"Let's make a secret society," Wyd suggested.

"You have to have a password and a badge," Jeff said.

"And a name," she added.

"What kind of name?"

"We have to call a secret meeting to decide what to call it," Wyd said, calling a secret meeting on the spot.

After a while, we settled on: 'The Secret Four.'

"Let's make badges," Jeff said.

"Yes! We can embroider an S and an F on them."

They found some colorful wool threads and sewed the initials on round pieces of blue cardboard, which they pinned to their shirts underneath their sweaters.

Wyd wrote in her book: "We have a secret society. We have a password. And a secret meeting. We also have a secret." She loved Enid Blyton stories.

"Better not write the secret in your book," I advised. "You still might like to show it to someone."

In addition to the password and badges, we had to have a secret knock. Wyd and Jeff agreed on three short knocks and two long.

"Don't let anyone in your cabin unless they give the secret knock," I said. "We'll start packing, but if anyone sees what we're doing they'll guess our secret. Let's make some piles of toys and clothes we can leave for kids on the junks."

The next morning we began sorting things. We tried to arrange it so as not to alert anyone should they intrude into the cabin. Everything was part of the Secret Society game, weaving excitement and fun into the situation. Fear hovered on the threshold of the cabin, but found no room inside.

After a while we stopped. Best to do only a bit each day. We had ten days to go.

"I'm going up on deck to clear the old lungs. Want to come?"

"I'm going to find Daddy," Jeff said. "There's time for a game of chess. "

"I'll come with you, Mummy. Don't ring the gong without me, Jeff."

"Okay. We'll meet in Stefan's pantry."

For a moment my heart sank. What if they thought it was a game? What if they failed to keep the secret absolutely? Did they understand its importance?

Gazing down at their shining, happy faces, my confidence returned. They understood the seriousness of a game better than I did. Wyd and I put on heavy jackets, wrapped long red wool scarves around our heads, and went outside. The sundeck was shrouded in cold, grey mist. Harold, all grey himself, leaned over the railing squinting at a destroyer that paralleled our course.

As it rose and fell in the strong waves, I could see it carried an American flag.

"Your friend is really dogging our footsteps," Harold said.

"People must be used to new ships by now. Let's walk, Wyd. It's too cold here."

Laughing breathlessly, we walked, relishing the wet and cold. When we went downstairs to get ready for lunch, Stefan was in the children's cabin, standing deep in thought over the empty bottom bureau drawer.

He turned around slowly.

"Hi, Stefan!" I said. "Brrrr, it's cold out. Wyd and I are sorting out summer clothes. Wyd said you can give some away to the boat-workers when we go back to Hong Kong. This pile over here. And these toys."

Without a flicker in his dark eyes, Stefan looked around at the changes in the cabin.

"A bit of a mess, isn't it?" I offered blandly. "But we'll straighten it out soon."

"Is it time to ring the gong?" Wyd asked, dropping her thick wool sweater on top of another pile of clothes on the couch.

Decades of despotism had taught Stefan the bitter rules of secrecy and conspiracy. He picked up his duster.

"Yes," he told Wyd. "Almost time."

29. NORTH PACIFIC

Storms Inside and Out

Aweek of North Pacific storms subdued everyone. We rarely encountered even crew members on the rain-slicked decks. Most of the passengers kept to their cabins. Bjorn was the only unquenched by the gloom on board. Dapper as ever, in his cheerfully colored polo neck sweaters and tight pants, he prowled the ship, irritating and amusing.

"Stefan tells me we're heading into a really big storm." He cornered me one afternoon when I was on deck. "You are a good sailor, Jane. You are not afraid to be outside. But it will get rougher."

"I like the fresh air."

"Do you see that?" He pointed across the ever-changing valleys and mountains of water at the destroyer. Its American flag flapped fiercely in the increasing force of the winds.

I shrugged: "It's been with us since we left Hong Kong."

"Ah, *mon ami*, it is amazing with your cleverness you are so naïve. Your compatriots across the water know more than you, obviously. He leaned out over the rail and looked up to make sure no one was listening on the overhead deck: "Your friend," he nodded at the destroyer, lowering his voice. "They have information."

"What about?" I asked, alert.

"The British were warned. That's why they cut the cotton bales. If I tell you what they were looking for, you will be in danger, as I am."

"From whom? The captain?"

"Of course," he said, as if to a child. "The captain will squash a person as easily as he does a fly."

Bjorn started to put his arm conspiratorially around my shoulders, then, as the ship smacked broadside against a wave, he grabbed the railing to steady himself.

"You are clever not to know, Jane. He has even tried to get me and I am from a neutral country. I am not an enemy like you."

He turned quickly, leading the way indoors. Wending his way toward his cabin, he held onto the long corridor banister. I was distressed by his unaccustomed awkwardness.

Our families were the only ones for lunch in the dining room. Stefan seemed cheered by our company. He told us funny tales from his youth, making us smile. The children talked happily to him as he served his vinegar-based meal designed to keep seasickness at bay. I stuck to thick slices of fresh bread and pickled red peppers. It worked for me. Afterwards, Alex, who ate everything and never got queasy, went back to his writing, while we went to the children's cabin. There Jeff and I did some surreptitious packing while Wyd read to us. I would leave one of our two trunks full of things for Stefan to share back home.

In the early afternoon it began to rain hard. It was already quite dark outside. Our vessel rocked and rolled in the dark-green immensity, the sea tossing us about in high spirits. Jeff and Wyd went with Alex into the lounge for a change of scene. Stefan came with the first mate to secure portholes. They locked the heavy steel and glass window part, then closed and bolted their round, solid steel outer covers. The mate gruffly reminded me that all doors must be kept shut, and loose objects stowed away.

"I already tell you we head for bad storm, Missus," Stefan said, looking worried. "Please, Missus, do not let the children go about alone. They must not go on deck at all. I tell Jeffy and Wyddy there is no gong tonight. I serve dinner in cabins for all passengers, at six o'clock."

"Okay. The kids are in the lounge with Alex now."

The only door to our deck left unlocked was the one at the far end of our corridor. I put on my thickest sweater and a yellow slicker. I had some trouble opening the door to the deck against the wind. Stepping outside, I found myself in the midst of an electrical storm. I had never seen anything like it. It was as if nature and sub-nature warred. Froth from enormous waves reached up to where I stood. The down-pouring rain was like needles. Thunder and lightning interspersed with phosphorescent trails on the roiling waters. Snake-like flames, about two feet high, shot up spasmodically, dancing erratically before dying suddenly away, leaving only dark. Firecracker snaps of the waves recreated the sounds of a naval battle. The play of eerie flickers on the ocean was almost continuous.

Speeding around like small boats, they seemed like phantom ships made of phosphorescent foam and dashes of electricity. There were no other ships to be glimpsed through the mist and cloud, not even the American destroyer.

A cold mountain of water hit broadside, causing Jessenice to tremble and tip sharply. I held onto a lifesaver until the ship straightened. Time to go back in. Reaching the passengers' door without mishap, I grabbed the door handle.

At that point I slipped and very nearly fell on the tilting, streaming deck.

"Missus, you all right?" Stefan had been just inside, supposedly closing the last porthole. He helped steady me while holding the door

211

open by pushing his back against it. I don't think I could have gotten inside without him.

I staggered in over the bulkhead. I'd never really noticed how high it was. Now I saw why: to keep out water. The wind closed the door with a bang.

"Missus, please!" His voice shook.

He did not say more. Nor did he need to.

I went to change out of my soaking-wet clothes. Later, I found Alex, Jeff, and Wyd in the lounge, playing cards. Most of the windows were shuttered tight, well covered. All the lights were on.

Alex looked at me without expression, but love was in his eyes, too.

"This is some storm," I said, excited. "It looks like a real battle out there."

The dining room was in darkness, and the front windows were not yet completely covered. Stefan had left the curtains open. I beckoned Alex and the children into the dark room, softly closing the lounge door behind us. The only illumination was a thin wedge of light from the pantry.

As we gazed at the magnificent storm, we imagined mischievous elementals pulling electricity from the ship's imprisoning wires to let their electric friends play freely for once atop the fiery phosphorescent waves.

Ten minutes later, returning to the lounge, we found Harold seated on the couch, and the captain's two giant sailors standing with their backs to the lounge door.

"You!" one of the sailors snapped, turning to face Alex as we entered. "Captain wish to see you."

We all tensed.

"Now! At once!"

Alex turned to me. I caught the warning in his eyes. I had a moment's longing for telepathy. What was he trying to tell me?

"Another one of the captain's whims, I suppose," he said, his back to the room. He leaned over the children, his big arms wrapping first Wyd, then Jeff in big hugs. Then, pantomiming a silly pretence that we were parting forever, he grabbed me, tipped me almost off balance, hugged and kissed me. We were both laughing. At the same time, so that the sailor could not see, he slipped his wallet into my jacket.

"I'm sure it won't take long. I'll join you for dinner in the cabin. See you, Harold. Bye, kids."

Impassive, the sailors parted to let Alex move between them, and then closed in behind him.

"What was that all about?" Harold asked.

"I don't know."

"What did Alex give you?"

"Nothing."

He turned away with a grunt. We stood for a minute, listening to the tempest. Even through the tightly closed windows we could hear the waves snapping like firecrackers in the wailing wind.

"It's enough to give anyone the willies," Harold said.

"Let's go back to our cabin," I signaled the children.

I hate the way grownups instill fear for no reason.

Locking the door, I took out Alex's wallet. Our passports were inside.

"Is Daddy safe?" Wyd asked, her face screwed with worry. Jeff's was white.

"Dad's all right," I hugged them both. "But we've got to hide our passports right away because we'll need them when we get off in Japan. Daddy slipped them to me before he left."

Reassured by this sign of his ingenuity, we looked around for a hiding place. Since the strongbox had been broken into once before, we passed it over now. My eyes rested on the large, fat souvenir books that the children were creating. There they were, right out in the open. Less likely to be guessed at as a hiding place, although probably not good enough if someone was intent on finding them. Still, for now, it was the safest place I could think of. As quickly as I could, I found scissors.

Without needing to be asked, Jeff opened his *Journey to Japan* to the back inside cover so I could slit between the beautiful, thick paper binding we had pasted as our inside cover, and slipped two passports side by side in between.

Then we did the same for the other two passports placing them as flat as possible, side by side, into Wyd's book. Then we glued the paper carefully back to the cover.

We stood silent with our own thoughts.

"I have to tell Stefan where Daddy is," I said to the children finally. Leaving them drawing pictures of ships in storms, I went to the pantry. Stefan was placing a large platter of baked potatoes on plates, preparing trays for the passengers' dinner.

"Is anything the matter?" he asked.

"Two sailors took Alex to the captain. I'm worried. I thought you should know."

"Mister be all right," Stefan kept on with his careful distribution of red peppers and crispy, thinly sliced pieces of iceberg lettuce. "Things are not what they seem." Then, in a low voice, he added: "Do not blame captain. He is good captain."

"Blame him?"

"I check now," Stefan said. "But please, Missus, stay in cabin tonight."

Even with his heartfelt plea ringing in my ears, I walked quickly down to the end of the long corridor, waiting there out of sight. Stefan emerged from the dining room shortly afterwards. His shirt was buttoned, his white jacket on. As I had hoped, he hurried halfway down the corridor to the inside stairs which led to the captain's quarters on the deck above. Once he was out of sight, I started back to the children's cabin. I had done what I could. Stefan would now do what he could.

I had just passed the stairs when a hard slap on my shoulder made me leap a foot off the carpet. My heart in my mouth, I turned to find myself face to face with Bjorn.

"Have you ever seen anything like this?" he said, waving toward the closed porthole at the end of the corridor.

"What the hell do you think you're doing?" I said, rubbing my stinging shoulder.

Bjorn's black eyes glittered. "Ah, you search for Alex, are you not?"

Whatever he had taken this time, it was too much.

He came closer. "Are you not afraid? I would not like to be Alex for anything."

"You're blathering! Why not?"

"Our captain, of course."

The ship lurched up a wave and slapped sickeningly down the other side. Bjorn held tightly to the banister. I deliberately refrained from holding on, balancing like a skier from the knees. His face was so close I could smell his sickeningly medicinal breath.

"We are smuggling shoulder-to-air missiles, Jane," he smirked triumphantly. "They are hand-held killers, the latest. I see by your face, now you understand. They were developed at the Skoda plant in Czechoslovakia. S.A.M.'s they call them. They are for Vietcong. If the Americans have discovered this they will blow our ship to tiny pieces. Everyone will assume it sank in the storm."

"S.A.M?" My mind was such a whirl I could only think of my brother, whose name was Sam. It seemed friendly.

Letting go of the railing, Bjorn swayed to the broken rhythm of the ship and again almost fell. "You are an intelligent woman. You know it is true."

A smart crack, louder than before, made us both jump. The lights went out.

"Aha! He has turned off lights!" Bjorn exulted, moving closer.

Almost at once the corridor was lit by the lurid red glow of emergency lights. I turned and left him quickly, hurrying back to the children's cabin. They were sitting together on Wyd's bed, Jeff's arm around his sister's shoulders, enveloped in the same dim glow.

Jeff gave me his place and went to try our secret knock to see if Alex were back. There was no answer. I gave him a hug, avoiding his worried eyes as I tried not to show that I was worried, too.

Bjorn's raving might mean nothing.

Still I couldn't stay inside, just waiting, any longer.

"Jeff, lock the door. Don't let anyone in but us when you hear the secret knock. Or Stefan."

I didn't want Bjorn wandering in on them in his present condition. Or anyone else, for that matter. Wyd settled on the bed with some books. As Jeff turned the lock, I heard Wyd begin to read aloud. I hurried off, grateful for their patience.

* * *

The rain had almost stopped, the wind had abated, the waves flattened, but the ship rolled and the deck was slick. Between the lightning and a few red emergency lights, I could see enough to get around our decks and the officers' deck. The eerie crackling sounds and sudden explosions coming from the sea were muted now, the ghostly green flares dimmer in the evening dark. The ship's wake was a curving snake's tail of shimmering phosphorescence.

Unable to resist, I went up another flight, keeping out of the gusty wind as much as possible. Then cautiously I climbed all the way up to the Star Deck.

Our American destroyer, all its lights blazing, was keeping pace. Sometimes its lights were bright on a mountain of black, sometimes it disappeared altogether as it shuddered into troughs of water. Was our darkened white ship as visible in the beautiful phosphorescence?

In any case, they would have us precisely located on their radar.

Spray needled my face as I went back down. Eerie flashes of blue lightning silhouetted the black shadows of the officers who stood grouped in the wheelhouse, the short, straight figure of the captain in their midst. Two of them were steadily surveying the American ship through binoculars. I imagined I could see the American officers watching back. The two ships were braided together by sinews of purpose and suspicion.

From the stairs I could also see Savo in his blinking and flashing room, working his splendid equipment with utter efficiency. Are the messages are finally interesting, Savo? I asked silently.

I backed down the steep bridge stairs, maneuvered the next slippery flight, trying to piece the puzzle together. I weaved against the wind, then, by edging along the spray-wet passenger deck from brass handhold to brass handhold, I circled back toward the one open door.

Ahead were two figures. One had slumped against the railing.

Seasick, no doubt. It looked as though the littler one was trying to help.

I came nearer and saw that the man's feet were no longer on deck. It seemed as if he were trying to jump. The other was preventing him. Or…the other way round?

"Hello!" I shouted, just in case. I held tightly to the railing as I struggled forward against the wind. "Can I help?"

The third mate, whom I was now near enough to recognize, jumped back, and the figure crumpled onto the deck. In the flash of lightning that followed, I made out Bjorn's inert form. Blood oozed from a crack in his forehead.

I kept my voice calm as I came near. "We'd better get him to his cabin."

"He be sick," the third mate said. "I try to help."

"Sure you did," I said, my voice neutral, trying not to retch.

"I go tell Captain."

"The man is hurt. Let's get him inside."

I was afraid he might roll overboard through the space under the railing. I was afraid the mate would leave me, and not come back.

"I tell Captain. You wait here." He hurried off.

I tried to pull Bjorn. Though not quite dead, he was dead weight, and too heavy for me to move by myself. Not trusting the third mate to report the accident, I left Bjorn lying in the rain. I had to tell someone. Desperation helped me pull hard enough to open the door against the wind. The corridor was still bathed in the lurid glow of emergency lights. I went first to the pantry. Stefan was not there. I hurried on to Grace's cabin. At my knock, Grace opened the door just a quarter, blocking entrance.

"What can I do for you?

"Bjorn's been hurt! He's out on deck. He needs to be looked at right away. His head's been cracked open."

"Oh, dear," Grace clucked her tongue. "Did you hit him?"

"Good God, no!" I stepped back to look at her. She was fully dressed in a long silk evening gown, a gold cigarette holder in a bejeweled left hand. The red lamps turned the folds of her white dress shades of pink, red and purple.

Arabella emerged from her cabin. "Is there anything wrong?"

"Jane says someone hit Bjorn," Grace said calmly, holding hard to the door against a sudden lurch of the ship.

"I did not!"

"If I were you, I would tell Stefan," Arabella said. "He's in charge of passengers."

"I don't know where Stefan is. We have to get Bjorn out of the rain."

"Ask Alex," Arabella suggested.

"I don't know where he is either."

"Why, honey, he's in your cabin with the children. I saw him go in just a short while back."

Without bothering to reply, I ran to our cabin. Alex was sitting on the couch, with Wyd and Jeff on his lap. They were holding on to him tightly. He was telling of his visit to the captain, making it sound reasonable and friendly. I threw myself on them and we tumbled over in a tangle, laughing with relief.

"I was wondering where you were," Alex looked at my wet clothes disapprovingly, yet with a twinkle of admiration in his eyes.

"Alex – we need your help."

"What's happened?" He got up, gently disentangling himself from the children.

"It's Bjorn. He's had some sort of accident to his head."

"Where is he?"

"Out on deck. I tried, but he's too heavy to move by myself. The third mate was there, but he left. Come on! Stay here, Kids. It's too dangerous right now on deck."

Once again they locked up behind us. Alex followed as I headed to the deck door. Before we reached it, we heard it thump open. Burly Savo, clutching Bjorn under the arms, roughly dragged his inert form over the high bulwark. He waited to be sure the door snapped shut, then clutching Bjorn by the heels, he continued bumping his burden along the corridor carpet like a sack of onions, growling us out of his way.

Grace waited beside her slightly opened door. Arabella was still standing in the corridor. When Grace made no move to let him in, the sailor lay the body down. Impassively, Grace surveyed Bjorn's crumpled form. In the sinister light of the blackout, his wet face was pink. The slash in his forehead was jet black. It was still slowly pulsing out blood. His mouth had fallen open, a black hole. His eyes were closed.

As she peered at Bjorn, Arabella leaned heavily on the sailor as if she might faint. "He looks ghastly. What happened?"

"I'll go find Stefan," I said. "Maybe he can do something."

"No. Take him inside my cabin, and put him on the far bed," Grace ordered the sailor. Then she placed a soft hand on my arm. "My dear, Stefan is not a nurse. I am. Don't you think I'm more qualified to look after my husband? The injury to his head needs special attention which only I know how to give." Her voice was a friendly monotone: "I'm fully capable of giving him stitches if they are required. I assure you I'm more capable than these sailors. I have all the medicines he needs. Really, Jane, don't bother Stefan now. We'll see how Bjorn is in the morning."

"He may be dead by morning!" I said.

Alex put a calming hand on my shoulder.

Grace glanced at Bjorn's limp form: "Oh, I think he'll be all right. He always did exaggerate the danger of a little bump to his head."

We turned away, going back to our corridor by way of the pantry. Stefan still wasn't there.

"There's really nothing we can do, if Grace doesn't want us to," Alex said.

We waited in the hall, wondering if Stefan would return.

"If Bjorn dies it's because he was murdered," I said.

"Don't talk so loud."

We both looked down the empty crimson corridor.

"Let's get back to the kids," Alex said.

Before we got there, we heard someone groan, then the sound of someone slipping. Turning, we saw a wildly disheveled Harold half slide down the inside stairs from the officers' deck.

Alex put his face up close and got the distraught man to focus on him. "What happened to you?"

Harold grabbed Alex's hands: "You've got to help me. It's Bjorn. He's lying somewhere on one of these blasted decks maybe with a crack in his skull and I can't find him!"

"It's all right!" Alex told him loudly, reaching through Harold's panic.

"But don't you see?" Harold's voice was high with hysteria. "I can't find him! He might be dead by now! Oh, God, I didn't mean to do it!"

"Harold, it's okay. He's okay!" Alex repeated.

"A sailor took him to his cabin. Grace says he's going to be all right," I put in.

Harold turned and clung to me. "What? Oh, Jane, will he really live?"

"Grace says there's no cause for alarm." I said. "I offered to fetch Stefan but she told me not to. She's going to take care of him."

"Oh, thank God!"

"You sure chose a wild night for a fight," Alex said.

Harold shook his head vehemently: "I didn't mean to do it. I wanted to find out what happened to our lights. I tried the deck door. Bjorn was outside, vomiting over the rail. I thought he needed help so I went out to him."

"Go on."

"He told me to bugger off. He didn't need my help. I left. He crept up behind me and – and hit me. Hard."

"He did?"

"Like a hard slap on the back," Harold corrected sheepishly. He hung his head. "It's my Commando training. I fought the Jerries from Calaise to the Rhine, and I'll never get over it. You learn how to deal with surprise attacks... I kept thinking I heard shellfire, too."

"Shellfire?"

"Yes. Didn't it seem to you that the Yank destroyer was firing at us?"

"Oh, the firecracker snaps of the waves," Alex said.

"I can't help it," Harold went on bitterly. "I hurt my own son once. He jumped at me from behind – a sort of joke. Playing at being a mountain lion or something. Then there was Jeff, you know. Oh, God, I tell you, it's a curse!"

"You knocked Bjorn out?"

Harold shook his head. "No, I just hit him. He slipped and fell. What if he dies?"

We were silent, wondering ourselves.

"It would be murder, wouldn't it?" Harold added.

"Not necessarily," Alex answered.

"Manslaughter, then. It's still a prison sentence. We have a captain who's a maniac."

"It's okay, Harold." Alex told him. "Nothing will happen before Japan. We won't tell anyone. We know it was an accident. Just don't talk about it."

Harold gripped Alex's hand. "You could have been born British, you're so damned decent! Not a bit like a Yank."

We accompanied Harold to his cabin. Bertha was outside, in her dressing gown, distraught. Stefan was with her. When she saw Harold, she clung to him sobbing. Stefan gently led them into their cabin, then came out, softly closing their door.

"I will bring them tea now," he said to us.

Arabella hovered nearby. "Have you heard there's been some trouble?" she told Stefan.

"Yes," I added. "I found Bjorn on deck with his head split open."

"He is hurt bad?"

"I think so. Grace says she can take care of him."

Arabella melted into her cabin without closing her door all the way.

"I could do with a drink," Alex said. "Stefan, would you get us one if we come with you?"

We walked to the lounge together in silence. Stefan poured slivovic for both of us, and then, for the first time, joined us by pouring a glass for himself as well. We stood talking, the storm still swaying us.

"Is it true," I asked him, "what Bjorn told me about some secret cargo?"

I noticed Stefan's hesitation only because I was waiting for it. It was infinitesimal.

"I know nothing about cargo, Missus."

"The American destroyer over there – do they know?"

"I pray not."

"Oh!" Alex said. "Now I begin to understand. The captain had me grabbed for questioning, thinking I might know something I shouldn't. He may even have suspected that I was in secret radio contact with the destroyer back there. But after a few minutes he changed his mind. I could tell the moment it occurred to him that I was a complete idiot."

"Why did you keep telling us the captain is a good man?" I asked Stefan.

"I say he is good captain," Stefan corrected. "I be responsible for passengers. Captain be responsible for ship and cargo."

"Captain thinks we are cargo."

"But you not be cargo. The children not be cargo. In Rijecka I report about passengers to authorities. Captain report only about ship. I do not like, but I remind Captain tonight. You be okay, Missus."

Alex gripped his long, thin hand. "Thank you, Stefan. You're a good friend."

"Good night, Mister. Goodnight Missus."

We both gave him a warm embrace.

30. THE SIDE OF SILENCE

We Escape

We waited all morning, wondering how to get off. Our luggage waited too, inside the locked cabin. Too much luggage, I thought, but there was no help for it. We were leaving behind everything that was not absolutely necessary. Even so, a large suitcase, a heavy typewriter, a large camera, full purse, plus the kids seemed too much to carry off nonchalantly.

At about two o'clock, Alex knocked our secret knock.

"The passengers are all in their cabins," he reported. "Grace has gone to a hospital with Bjorn. The first mate went with them. No one else is allowed ashore. It's captain's rest hour. I can hardly believe it, but the gangplank is lowered and there's no sign of crew. Probably too far out to need guards. I can't see with this fog. I'm going to try to signal a passing boat. Wish me luck."

He picked up the odd yellow cane he'd the monk in Elephanta had given him.

"Just what you need now," I grinned back, picking up on Alex's courage. "No one will be able to tell whether you're coming or going."

He smiled his big reassuring smile for the children, then left. I locked the door after him and returned to the porthole. The currents being highly treacherous, few small boats braved the swirling grey waters. I tried to ease the tension by getting the children to recite *The Owl and the Pussy Cat*. Should anyone be listening at the door they would not guess that we were actually waiting to make our escape.

Forty-five long minutes passed before Alex knocked again.

"I have a boat," he said, quickly. "Don't be upset when you see it. Best I could do. We have to hurry."

I paled perceptibly when I saw the low-slung dinghy thrashing wildly in the choppy waves around the freighter. There was no way we could all fit in.

The boatman screamed at what seemed to him mountains of luggage. "Ayee! No!"

"Better move fast," Alex ordered, bounding down the gangplank to catch him before he could push off. Waves were propelling the fragile craft into the ship's steely side. Alex grabbed a rope and knotted it around the railing of the gangplank, anchoring the dinghy to its precarious perch. I stayed at the top with the luggage and the kids.

"No! No!' groaned the terrified owner. "Break boat!"

I waited for Alex's signal, then, when he gave it, I turned to the children. "Stay here, Jeff, Wyd. Don't move, okay? I'll be right back."

I grabbed the big suitcase – the one containing the children's scrapbooks – and stepped onto the precariously slippery gangplank. Keeping close to the white flank of the ship, I managed to bring the piece to the wet bottom stair. Alex took it and threw it into the tiny boat.

"Forget the luggage," shouted Alex. "Get the kids."

I climbed back up, panting for breath. It was about two flights. I took Wyd by the hand and smiled encouragingly at Jeff: "I'll be right back," I promised. "It's too slippery to go by yourself."

Holding Wyd's hand tightly, I made my way down to the heaving, thrashing boat. Alex lifted Wyd aboard, a combination lift and jump. A wave hit the boat at the same moment. They both fell at one end of the dinghy. Cold water splashed in.

"I go!' The terrified boatmen leapt for the rope.

From his crouching position in front of Wyd, Alex waved his fantastical cane.

"Stay where you are!" he roared furiously.

The man cowered back onto a seat. "You crazy!" he shouted.

Alex seized a boathook. Pushing with all his strength, he kept the fragile vessel clear of the freighter's side. The boatman helped him.

I ran up the stairs again to get Jeff, moving without any will of my own. A tall shadow blocked the top step. Gasping, I clung to the railing.

"Why you take so much?" It was Stefan, white and shaking.

Two giant sailors loomed behind him. I met his angry eyes with my own. I kept mine friendly.

"We're going overland, Stefan. I left all our things in the cabin." My voice was breathless, but my inner turmoil was controlled so the sailors, who could not understand English, would not get suspicious.

"We'll meet you in Yokohama."

It was an offering, a small offering, something which he could use to explain to the captain. Jeff was behind Stefan. I followed his frightened gaze for his sister in the tiny boat far below. I saw Alex grimly fighting the wind and waves, which the terrified boatman longed to flee. I knew what I was asking of Stefan. There was nothing I could do to help him, if he decided to help us now.

"You wait," Stefan ordered. "I tell Captain."

He signaled the sailors, who closed in at the railing, one on either side of the gangplank. They watched, on guard. I put out my hand to touch the lapel of his jacket. My eyes held his, as his had held mine once before in Aden. There was no time for words to pass, memories to well up, kindness to infuse. There was no time to explain, apologize, to beg. Yet something passed between us.

"My friend, not right now."

Stefan stepped backwards. My hand fell limply to my side. He took another step. Then he stopped. His shiny old clothes pulled sideways by the wind, snapped loudly. His voice was barely audible: "I help with Jeff." The lightning speed of our thoughts had vanished; we were back in ordinary space-time.

"Thank you," I said, my eyes full. "I know what this means. I'll make sure the children understand some day what you have done for them."

Stefan leaned his long awkward body to take Jeff in his arms. Tenderly he smiled his sad, black and white smile as he skillfully carried him down the slippery gangplank.

Without looking at the sailors who still stood like statues by the rail, I picked up the camera and the typewriter. Half way down, I met Stefan coming up. I could not give more than the small comfort of a grateful look for fear he might reveal himself to the two sailors above. Was it spray or tears on his face?

Moving quickly, I fell onto the seat beside Jeff. Cursing, the boatman pushed off. The dinghy twisted capriciously as he fought free of the currents.

"Jeff! Wyd! Goodbye!"

The children looked up. Stefan stood at the top of the gangplank. White hair and white coat gleamed against the duller white of the freighter. He stretched out his long, bony arms and waved. For a moment it looked as if he could reach the distance and embrace us all.

Mists curled and billowed around him like friendly wraiths. He became dimmer, a ghost on his own ghostly ship. Fog thickened, enfolding him until he was barely a wavering outline. Then there was only soft, thick silence all around.

EPILOGUE

Solid Laughter

Wrapping ourselves in experience, blankets around our souls, we move on.

The choppy harbor water subsided to smooth swells as we neared our landing. The boatman subsided into annoyed silence and stroked smoothly. We landed without further argument or anguish. We gave our thanks, plus something extra to make it worth his while, and parted amicably.

Struggling under the weight of our luggage, we were silently directed to the entrance of the customs house, a noble edifice, purposefully imposing, and effectively intimidating for disembarking passengers in our situation.

Without explanations we were led into an enormous room lined with a long, desk that curved across its entire space at our end. The space curved up to a brightly-lit ceiling. Behind the desk, that reached above our heads, there were lined nine scribes, each busy with other passengers and their papers.

The rest of the floor was filled with quiet employees writing at their desks, studiously ignoring the unease of the incoming passengers.

"Come here!" One of the customs officials waved us over. "Why you bring so much luggage?"

"Sir, we are asking for asylum," Alex replied.

"Why you shake?"

"We have just escaped from that Yugoslav freighter just anchored off-shore. We ask your permission to land in Japan."

Alex bowed respectfully and we waited in silence.

Our interrogator spent time discussing the situation in Japanese with several colleagues gathered around him. To our surprise and relief, they all began to smile as they spoke. Then he called us to his attention.

"When you get off Yugoslaahve freighter," he said, laughing, "You shake like you." He proceeded to demonstrate his point shaking hands and arms vigorously and laughing gleefully. Then becoming more decorous, he added: "Please be guest in our country. You may stay as long as you wish. Taxis take you to your hotel."

With a flourish and a smile, he stamped our visas and passports. Handing each back to its proper owner, even the children, he exchanged polite chuckles with each of us in turn.

We smiled and laughed also, deeply thankful for this wonderful, open invitation.

Alex and I looked at each other with deep understanding. We felt affirmed in the secret purpose of our entire journey: we had wanted our children to know that the whole world is their garden. We wanted them now to know, too, that it is theirs to care for, as so many others had cared for them.

Still accompanied by much laughter now, including from the fellow scribes still seated upon their lofty heights, we were led outside to a nearby taxi stand.

Walking, we noted a new, very odd feeling which at first tipped us off balance: we were no longer automatically going up and down to the rhythm of the waves.

We now had to rebalance ourselves to the unaccustomed rhythms of dry land.

ABOUT THE AUTHOR

Writer, traveler, educator, Jane Winslow Eliot's articles and essays have appeared in *The Atlantic, Smithsonian, Horticulture, Travel & Leisure, Newsday, The Los Angeles Reader,* and *Chicken Soup for the Traveler's Soul.*

Her books range from seminal essays for parents and teachers such as *Let's Talk, Let's Play* (AWSNA Publications 1997) to *The History of the Western Railroads* (Bison Books 1985*)*, and *Fisher's Annotated Guide to Greece 1984 -1988.* She is also a contributor to the *Almanac of American History.* A film made with her husband, Alexander Eliot, *The Secret of Michelangelo – Every Man's Dream,* appeared on primetime ABC in 1967-68.

CPSIA information can be obtained
at www.ICGtesting.com
Printed in the USA
LVOW13s0513210718
584518LV00008B/81/P